W9-AFX-301

THE BOOK
OF
MERLIN

Merlin – magician, kingmaker and prophet – remains one of the most fascinating and intriguing figures of legend.

The Merlin Conference held in London on 14th June, 1986 was the first of a series of annual events to discuss, explain and decipher the character, influence and prophecy of this powerful and evocative figure. With Merlin as a central theme, the Conference ranged over history, legend, drama, psychology, story-telling, folklore, music, magic, prophecy, mysticism, literature and film. Merlin's lessons were, after all, carried by tales, songs, poems and tradition, not merely by literary texts alone.

Each of the contributors is an international expert in his own right, having previously published material on Merlin and the legends of Arthur. As a non-commercial event, the annual Merlin Conference aims to generate interest in the mysterious figure of Merlin, to renew neglected traditions and offers a wide spectrum of information, performance and discussion.

The *BOOK OF MERLIN*, edited by R. J. Stewart and illustrated by Miranda Gray, is based upon that first significant and memorable event. It includes new research, insights and invaluable studies of the true nature of Merlin through the centuries: *Merlin in the Earliest Records* by Geoffrey Ashe; *Merlin in Fiction* by John Matthews; *Merlin as an Archetype* by Gareth Knight; *Merlin, King Bladud and the Wheel of Life* by Bob Stewart; Thomas Heywood's *Chronographical History*; William Shakespeare's *The Birth of Merlin*; Ranulph Higden's *Polychronicon*; Geoffrey of Monmouth's *Prophecies* and *Life of Merlin*.

There are also items on Merlin in magical arts and poetry, Merlin and sexuality in legend and tradition, the blue stones of Preseli and much more.

THE BOOK OF MERLIN

Insights from the First Merlin Conference, London, June 1986

Edited by R. J. Stewart

BLANDFORD

First published in the UK 1987 by Blandford Press
an imprint of Cassell
Artillery House, Artillery Row,
London SW1P 1RT

Reprinted 1989
(Paperback edition 1988)

Copyright © 1987 R. J. Stewart

Distributed in the United States by
Sterling Publishing Co, Inc,
387 Park Avenue South, New York, NY 10016–8810

Distributed in Australia by
Capricorn Link (Australia) Pty Ltd
PO Box 665, Lane Cove, NSW 2066

British Library Cataloguing in Publication Data

Merlin Conference *(1st : 1986 : London)*
   The book of Merlin.   1.Merlin—Legends—
History and
   criticism
   I.Title   II. Stewart, R.J.
   398'.352   PN686.M4
XXX

ISBN 0 7137 1945 1 (Hardback)
ISBN 0 7137 2078 6 (Paperback)

All rights reserved.
No part of this book may be reproduced
or transmitted in any form or by any means,
electronic or mechanical, including photocopying,
recording or any information storage and
retrieval system, without permission
in writing from the Publisher.

Printed and bound in Great Britain by
Mackays of Chatham PLC, Chatham, Kent

Contents

5

CONTENTS

List of Contributors

The main chapters of this book are arranged in alphabetical order, which curiously happened to be an excellent order in terms of the material delivered by each speaker or author.

Geoffrey Ashe is the author of a number of books on Arthurian subjects, and an internationally known lecturer. His books include: *King Arthur's Avalon, Quest for Arthur's Britain, Guidebook to Arthurian Britain, Avalonian Quest, Gandhi (*biography*), The Finger and the Moon (*novel*)* and *The Ancient Wisdom*. He is also associate editor of the major *Arthurian Encyclopedia*.

Dr Gareth Knight has been actively working with Western esoteric traditions for over 30 years. His books include: *A Practical Guide to Qabalistic Symbolism, The Secret Tradition in Arthurian Legend, The Rose Cross and the Goddess* and *The Treasure House of Images*.

John Matthews: author of *The Grail; Quest for the Eternal, The Western Way (*2 vols*), At the Table of the Grail* (editor), and *Warriors of Arthur* (with R. J. Stewart). John Matthews and Caitlin Matthews have jointly written and taught on many aspects of British and Celtic tradition.

Bob Stewart: R. J. Stewart is author of *The Prophetic Vision of Merlin, The Mystic Life of Merlin* and *The UnderWorld Initiation* which deal in depth with traditions of prevision and psychic transformation. He is also author of a number of books on folklore, Romano-Celtic culture, music and the elemental psyche, plus children's stories and adult fiction. Editor of the *Book of Merlin*, he is a composer and musician working in theatre, television, and film.

Miranda Gray illustrated the *Book of Merlin*, and has also recently published the colour cover for *Living Magical Arts* by Bob Stewart. She is currently working on a major full colour Tarot project for publication in 1988.

Acknowledgements

The Editor wishes to acknowledge the work undertaken by those who contributed to the First Merlin Conference and helped to make it such an outstanding success; in addition to the team of stewards who enabled the event to happen, specific acknowledgement is due to the following individuals: Mary Stutters, Caitlin Matthews and Jonathon Lane. Also to Denise Coffey for reading and discussing 'The Birth of Merlin'.

Individual contributors to the book are credited in the list of contents, but an overall acknowledgement must be made to the many people who corresponded, telephoned, discussed, advised and argued about the figure of Merlin.

The final acknowledgement, of course, must be duly given to Merlin himself.

R. J. Stewart, 1987

Introduction

The book which follows is drawn primarily from papers presented at the First Merlin Conference, held in London in 1986. Even if the Conference had been poorly attended, these contributions from a variety of authors and experts would have made a worthy publication; but the Conference was filled to capacity and many people were turned away.

Within a decade or so, Merlin has reappeared in the collective imagination as a serious figure – which does not mean that he is devoid of humour, but that people are seriously re-assessing the traditions represented by him.

In brief, Merlin is a primal seer, bard, or prophet of the British land; yet his traditions enfold Europe, and therefore also have some validity for America and Australia, not in a sense of quaint antiquarianism or mere romance, but as a potent source of imagery and inspiration stemming from enduring cultural roots. There are a number of curious qualities about the figure of Merlin which are worthy of our attention. He is a figure from the collective imagination, associated with pagan philosophical and magical practices, but, unlike King Arthur and his knights with whom he eventually became associated through fiction, he extends timelessly beyond the limits of 'racial' definition. Merlin is a prophet of Britain; but he is not limited to a historical or racial British context; his wisdom is transpersonal, and therefore transcultural.

In the East there are many well defined figures who embody powerful ancient traditions of wisdom that still fuse cultural and personal growth together. In the West such figures were corrupted or vilified by political religion; and when potent images such as those of Arthur, his warriors, his court, and his code of honour, are forcibly separated from a genuine religion, overview, or practical flow of traditional education, they can become dangerous stereotypes. Merlin, however, is the British version of the magician, seer, hermit,

9

shaman or medicine man found in every culture worldwide. The similarities between texts such as the *Prophecies of Merlin* and the *Life of Merlin* and American Indian lore cannot be denied, though there is no suggestion here that Merlin was really an American Indian!

There are certain primal modes of consciousness discernible in the relationship between humankind and the land, or environment. These are prevalent in shamanistic magic, and much of this type of tradition is clearly present in the figure of Merlin. But Merlin also deals with a complex harmonious cosmology, and certain definitions of the human psyche which predate modern psycho-analysis by many centuries, yet undeniably reveal many of the same insights. There is, however, a great deal of difference between magical psychology such as that demonstrated by Merlin, and modern materialist psychology which has been intellectually assembled without any traditional foundation or cosmic overview. The universality of the Merlin tradition is founded upon a vision of existence in which humankind, the land, the planet, the solar system and ultimately the stars all have a relationship to one another.

The shamanistic Merlin teaches us about human relationships with the land in the culture of our ancestors, while the refined wisdom of the aged Merlin moulds this primal set of relationships into an overview. There are also clear indications of transpersonal powers of consciousness in Merlin legends: the famous *Prophecies* are not merely trick verses concocted by Geoffrey of Monmouth, they are the literary recreation of an oral tradition of visionary experience, and even include the means whereby such visions are attained. In other words there is no spurious racial superiority in Merlin, but a strong emphasis upon personal transformation; this is particularly well developed in the *Vita Merlini*, a text which was virtually unknown other than to specialist scholars until quite recently. While politicians may abuse Arthur as a symbol of 'purity', Merlin reminds us constantly, in his *Life* and his *Prophecies* and associated later legends that humankind is weak, woeful; and that far from being a glorious and superior land, Britain is to be subjected to an increasing downward spiral of problems due to a failure to recognise truth. In Christian mystical terminology this is the allegory of the Grail and the Waste Land,

which may be both personal, collective, and nati mal or even international in manifestation, though spiritual in essence. In the simpler
language of the pagan Celtic root imagery, the land and the people
become separated from one another, and every ill results from this
separation. Merlin, therefore, is a significant bridging figure between
pagan and Christian concepts, and between European and world
traditions of magical, mystical, and spiritual development.

This book is divided into five sections, each including a main
chapter dealing with Merlin and related subjects, with a number of
short items which support or throw light on the main subject-matter.

The choice of contents has been difficult; for after the com-
missioned chapters from Geoffrey Ashe, Gareth Knight, John Matthews, and myself, a monumental bulk of material relating to Merlin
had to be considered. There is a popular misconception that after
examining early chronicles and Celtic sources, there is little to be
found on Merlin other than in the developments of relatively modern
fiction. This is simply untrue, and to redress the misconception, I
have included examples of early examinations and fictional presentations of Merlin and related subjects. These are:

Polychronicon, by Higden in a metrical translation by John Trevisa.
Life of Merlin by Thomas Heywood which merges scholarly analysis with
rampant story-telling.
The Birth of Merlin, a play reputedly written by Shakespeare and adapted by
William Rowley in the seventeenth century.
Barinthus, an important article from the *Revue Celtique* by A. Brown, which
returns us to an academic atmosphere, and sheds light upon some of the subjects
dealt with by our other contributors.

In this first assembled *Book of Merlin* we have set out to correct some
of the arrant nonsense recently attached to the figure of Britain's
primal prophet ... he is not a stereotyped old man with a star
spangled hat, nor is he some vapid 'New Age' pseudo-master who
will cure all ills and disburse wisdom to us willy nilly. Exactly who
and what Merlin is is suggested and researched in the following pages,
and demonstrated through both fact and fiction.

It is interesting to discover that one cannot write about Merlin without expressing oneself in certain enduring techniques for changing consciousness; these may be myth and legend, or the more detailed teachings found in books such as the *Vita Merlini*. Merlin is associated with seership, therapy, astrology, psychology, spiritual maturity, sexual emancipation, environmental relationship, and the vast body of ancient lore handed down from Celtic and druidic culture. But he also reaches far into the future as a prophet associated with apocalyptic imagery, and as a being who is at once human and transhuman.

Merlin is also inseparable from the image and power of a Goddess; and this relationship is vital for the present day, for the Goddess represents the land, the planet, and balancing feminine consciousness. In more immediate terms, Merlin exemplifies a cycle of relationships between male and female ... this real Merlin is far removed from the mono-sexual demonic elder fabricated by Victorian fantasy. One of the main topics of the 1987 Merlin Conference is 'Merlin and Woman', and a further *Book of Merlin* will include the material that develops from this theme.

PART 1
MERLIN IN THE EARLIEST RECORDS

Poly-Olbion

'Of Merlin and his skill what region doth not hear?
The world shall still be full of Merlin everywhere.
A thousand lingering years his prophecies have run,
And scarcely shall have end till time itself be done
Who of a British nymph was gotten, whilst she played
With a seducing spirit, which won the godly maid:
(As all Demetia through, there was not found her peer)
Who, being so much renown'd for beauty far and near,
Great lords her liking sought, but still in vain they prov'd:
By that spirit (to her unknown) this virgin only lov'd
Which taking human shape, of such perfection seem'd
As (all her suitors scorn'd) she only him esteem'd,
Who, feigning for her sake that he was come from far,
And richly could endow (a lusty bachelor)
On her that prophet got, which from his mother's womb
Of things to come foretold until the general doom.'

Michael Drayton
From: *Poly-Olbion* p 210, Col.1, Song V

Introduction
by R. J. Stewart

One of the many curious aspects of Merlin in the nineteenth and twentieth centuries is that everyone knew all about him ... yet hardly anyone took the trouble to examine the relationship between this assumed popular literary knowledge, and the genuine sources, origins and nature of the character of Merlin.

This dichotomy led to the appearance of a horribly imbalanced and often comical figure ... the doddering old man in a funny costume, or the sexually imbalanced elder who falls from wisdom and grace through the seductive wiles of a young nymph. More recently we have a fringe element of Merlin as a type of 'spirit guide' or 'guru', and this quaintly English type of nuttiness is perhaps the most pernicious of all. If we need to lay any blame for such wanderings, it should, perhaps, be attributed to the nineteenth-century occultists who assembled vast literary systems based upon Eastern and Hebrew orthodoxy mixed with Renaissance theosophy, yet hardly bothered to consider their native traditions at all. Thus we have today a bizarre situation in which modern students of ancient traditions of wisdom in the West draw upon purely literary creations, and are even taught that these are 'magical traditions'.

While the Victorian edifices of pseudo-symbolism were being assembled, however, another body of diligent researchers delved into Celtic culture and Celtic studies in early literature and language. This work is of a very different nature, and provided the foundation for many recent insights into the mythology, psychology, and symbolism of early texts, legends, characters, and, of course, the monumental body of Arthurian lore.

Somehow, the two extremes of wildly speculative systematic symbolism and extremely dry literary research must fuse and transform one another; the figure of Merlin acts as an effective focus for this alchemical process. Before proceeding with any of the detailed traditions found in texts from the sixth to the thirteenth century, we need to reassess the origins of Merlin himself.

As Geoffrey Ashe shows, these origins are complex and perhaps surprising ... but as Merlin was born of a human mother and an otherworld or transhuman father, we should expect only the unexpected when we examine the earliest records.

Merlin in the Earliest Records
by Geoffrey Ashe

To speak of the 'earliest records' in connection with Merlin is to encounter an instant difficulty. With documents of the classical age, or of modern times, we can usually fix a date – more or less – and determine what is early and what is not. With the presentation of Merlin to the world, we are in a realm of uncertainties. This is the case with most delvings into Celtic antiquity. Writings which are not very early themselves are apt to be the only sources for myths and traditions from a remote era and fragments of genuine history. Sometimes, we can be fairly confident in picking out such embedded items and, thereby, working backwards into the past. But the reason for undertaking this exercise may well be that no actual early records survive. In that case, we are trying, in effect, to reconstitute what they would have said, and while this can be a valid procedure, the age and authenticity of the items we work with may be hard to establish. In this perplexing field of study, I have no choice but to follow the judgment of professional scholars, reserving the right to explore beyond, but stressing that such exploration may be very conjectural indeed.

First let me map a course. With Merlin it is no use going straight to the few fairly early materials and trying to sift their testimony as to what is earlier still. We shall only be able to make sense of them if we are clear what we are talking about; what kind of ancient roots we are seeking; and that means starting with Merlin's début as a recognisable character whose roots can be sought. From there, we can take our backward steps in time, two or three of them, maybe more. But first we have to know where 'there' is.

His début occurs in the work of a highly inventive medieval author, Geoffrey of Monmouth. Geoffrey has been spoken of as Merlin's creator. That is true in a sense, but misleading. It could similarly be said that Geoffrey created King Arthur. True again, but misleading again, because this is *not* the kind of creation we mean if we say, for example, that Dickens created Mr Pickwick. Geoffrey's Arthur is not a wholly fictitious figure conjured by literary imagination out of nothing. He is a character developed from older tradition, which seems, indeed, to have its origin in a real person – perhaps more than one, but one anyhow. The same applies to Geoffrey's Merlin. He, likewise, is not a total fabrication. But his antecedents are at least as puzzling as King Arthur's, and the 'earliest records', as far as we can get hold of them, have somewhat the air of a three-card trick. Perhaps that is appropriate.

GEOFFREY OF MONMOUTH

To begin with, a little needs to be said about Geoffrey himself. He was a twelfth-century cleric of Welsh or possibly Breton descent. His home town of Monmouth is in south-east Wales, but between 1129 and 1151 he was a teacher at Oxford, where schools already existed, although the University did not. He moved to London and in 1152 was consecrated Bishop of the Welsh See of St Asaph (but probably never went there) and died two or three years later.

Geoffrey wrote three books, all in Latin, the learned and international language of his day. The first, composed in the early 1130s, was called *The Prophecies of Merlin.* Merlin was a theme of his writing from the beginning of his career as an author. But Geoffrey was not yet portraying Merlin as a character. He had simply picked up a name that was already attached to mantic Welsh verse, and had then produced a series of alleged prophecies under that name. The bulk of these he made up himself, though he claimed to have translated them from 'the British tongue' – here presumably meaning Welsh, though in another place in his work it probably means Breton. The book of *Prophecies*, as a volume in itself, exists in manuscript copies but not in an accessible printed form. However, the ordinary reader can still study it, incorporated into the text of a much greater book on which Geoffrey was already working, his masterpiece *The History of the Kings of Britain*. As the *Prophecies* now appear within

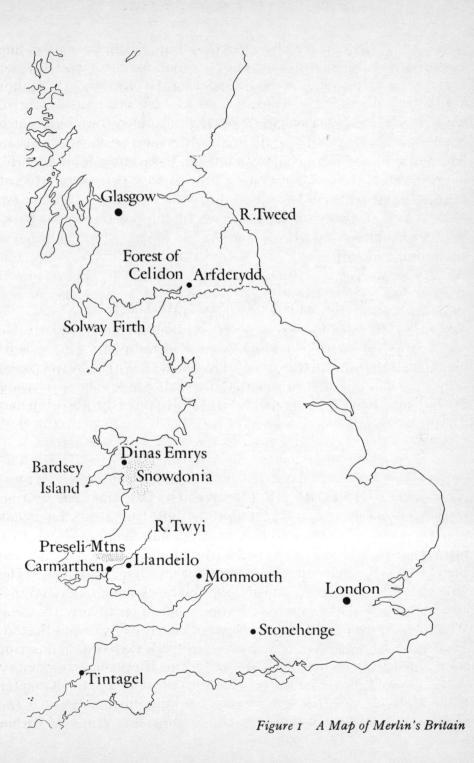

Glasgow

R.Tweed

Forest of
Celidon Arfderydd

Solway Firth

Dinas Emrys
Bardsey   Snowdonia
Island

R.Twyi

Preseli Mtns
Carmarthen Llandeilo
Monmouth
London

Stonehenge

Tintagel

Figure 1   A Map of Merlin's Britain

that setting, they cover a stretch of time that begins soon after what is assumed to be the date of Merlin's uttering them, in the fifth century AD, and runs on to the twelfth century and into an indefinite future.

Some of the prophecies can be related to actual events; mostly, of course, events that had already 'fulfilled' them when Geoffrey wrote. The majority are cryptic and can be read variously. Many medieval commentators throughout western Europe took them seriously and tried to interpret them.

Whatever Geoffrey's intention when he composed the *Prophecies*, it was soon subordinated to another: the portrayal of the prophet himself in a historical context. He did this in the course of the same *History of the Kings of Britain*, which he completed about 1136. It became one of the major books of the Middle Ages, laying the groundwork for the whole vast scheme of Arthurian romance, and supplying themes for Spenser, Shakespeare, and many more. Geoffrey's line of alleged kings begins with Brutus, who settled Britain in the aftermath of the Trojan War with a company of migrating Trojans, and ends with Cadwallader in AD 689. It is in the *History* that King Lear enters literature, and it is in the *History* that Merlin, as we know him, does likewise.

THE HISTORY OF THE KINGS OF BRITAIN

The History of the Kings of Britain is an extraordinary book. There is nothing else quite like it. Though not history, it is not pure fiction either, except in some of the early passages. Geoffrey undoubtedly uses history, or what he takes to be history; he draws on Roman and British authors, distorting and inflating and romanticising their testimony, yet seldom entirely losing touch with it. While we can never trust any passage in the book as it stands, we can often see what the materials were that went into it, and what actual people he is talking about or basing characters upon. When he is dealing with famous Romans, there is generally no problem. Julius Caesar as presented in the *History* is simply a fictionalisation of the actual man, who is amply attested in reliable documents. We can examine these and thus appraise what Geoffrey says. But when he moves into the half-light of Celtic legend, and tells (for instance) of Arthur and Guinevere, the searching-out of the matter in which he found their originals, its evaluation as history or legend or myth, and the final assessment of his creative feat, will be a much more formidable task. Such a task has to be faced when he introduces Merlin.

The setting of the story is the fifth century, some years before Arthur's birth. Geoffrey has told how the usurping British king Vortigern allowed the heathen Saxons, ancestors of the English, to settle in Britain as auxiliary troops. Thousands more, he says, followed the first contingent. Their leader Hengist dominated Vortigern and massacred the chief British nobles, and the Saxons overran parts of the country. Thus far, Geoffrey's picture of national misfortune is not completely divorced from real history. But now it becomes more fanciful. Vortigern, he continues, fled to Wales and tried to build himself a fortress in Snowdonia. His workmen laid the foundations, but the building materials kept vanishing. The king's magicians told him that he must find a boy without a father, kill him, and sprinkle his blood over the site. Only then would the subsidence halt and the foundations hold firm.

Vortigern sent out messengers to search through the land. In a town later called Carmarthen, his messengers heard a lad taunting another with never having had a father. The victim was Merlin. It transpired that his mother was a princess and was living in a nearby convent. She and her son were brought before Vortigern, and she told him she had conceived by intercourse with a being in human form, who, however, appeared and disappeared and was evidently not human. In mythological terms, he was an incubus.

Satisfied that the lack of a human father fulfilled the condition, Vortigern prepared for the sacrifice. However, Merlin told him that the magicians' advice was worthless because they did not know what they were talking about – and he would prove it. He challenged them to explain what was under the foundations and had caused their collapse. They had no idea. He predicted to the king that excavation would reveal a pool underneath; and so it did. Then he asked the magicians what was at the bottom of the pool. Again they had no idea. Merlin declared that if the pool was drained, two dragons would appear; so they did. One was red, the other was white. They fought, and at first the white dragon had the advantage, but presently the red recovered and drove it back.

Overawed, Vortigern spared Merlin and asked what the battle of the dragons portended. Merlin wept, went into a trance, and explained that the red dragon stood for the Britons and the white for the Saxons, who, because of Vortigern, were afflicting Britain. A grim ordeal lay ahead, hence his tears, but the Britons would recover and counter-attack.

This is where Geoffrey inserts Merlin's prophecies, following on from the interpretation of the dragons. The series begins with a reference to the current troubles and the coming triumphs of Arthur, who will, for the moment, end them. It goes on to many things that are more obscure. One plain forecast is that the Britons – meaning their Welsh, Cornish and Breton descendants, supported by other Celts – will rise to ascendancy again, seemingly after Geoffrey's time, and the ancient dynasty of the founder Brutus will reign supreme. England will cease to be called England and become once more Britain, a Celtic realm. Or, as Geoffrey makes Merlin put it:

'Cadwallader shall summon Conanus and shall make an alliance with Albany. Then the foreigners shall be slaughtered and the rivers will run with blood. The mounts of Armorica shall erupt and Armorica itself shall be crowned with Brutus' diadem. Kambria shall be filled with joy and the Cornish oaks shall flourish. The island shall be called by the name of Brutus and the title given to it by the foreigners shall be done away with.'

In the *History*, after delivering himself of this and much else, Merlin reverts to the immediate situation and foretells that Vortigern will be slain by Britain's rightful princes, Aurelius Ambrosius and Uther. It duly happens, and Aurelius becomes king. He bring the Saxons more or less under control and executes Hengist.

Merlin, introduced as a boy, seems to mature very rapidly. He appears next when Aurelius summons him to the court, to advise on a memorial for the nobles whom Hengist massacred, and who lie buried in a mass grave near Salisbury. Aurelius invites Merlin to prophesy the future, but he declines, for an interesting reason:

'Mysteries of that sort cannot be revealed except where there is the most urgent need for them. If I were to utter them as an entertainment, or where there was no need at all, then the spirit which controls me would forsake me in the moment of need.'

As to the proposed monument he is more helpful. He suggests bringing over a great circle of stones, called the Giants' Ring, from Ireland. Aurelius sends him with an expedition headed by Uther. They are unable to shift the stones, but Merlin uses his arts (which are not specified) to dismantle the circle. The stones are shipped to Britain and he places them over the nobles' grave ... and that is how Stonehenge came to be there. Later, three kings are buried in the same place.

Merlin is called upon again to expound a portent that appears in the sky, while Uther is marching against a confederation of Saxons and other enemies. As on the previous occasion, he sheds tears, this time because he knows that Aurelius has just died, and summons his familiar spirit. He forecasts that Uther will be victorious and reign over Britain, and will have a powerful son – a second foreshadowing of Arthur.

His final exploit concerns Arthur again and is his most notorious deed in the *History*. Uther pacifies the realm and, as king, holds a banquet in London. Among the guests are Gorlois, Duke of Cornwall, and his beautiful wife Ygerna. Uther is seized with ungovernable desire for her. His attentions are obvious, and Gorlois, without permission, leaves the court taking her with him. Uther treats this act as an insult and sends troops to ravage the ducal lands in Cornwall. Gorlois immures his wife in the castle of Tintagel, which can only be entered by a narrow isthmus, easily guarded. Assuming that she is out of Uther's reach, he hurries off to take charge of his army.

Uther seeks Merlin's aid. Here Merlin uses explicit magic, apparently for the first time, since we have not been told how he handled the megaliths. He transforms Uther into an exact replica of the Duke. Thus effectively disguised, Uther goes to Tintagel, where the guards allow him to pass, under the impression that he is Gorlois. Ygerna supposes likewise. Uther spends the night with her and begets Arthur. The real Gorlois has just fallen in battle with the royal troops, so Uther is able to resume his true likeness and make Ygerna his queen.

This is almost the last occasion in the *History* on which Merlin is mentioned. Geoffrey has made him prepare the ground for Arthur, and even contrive his conception. Yet, surprisingly in the light of later developments, they never meet. Much later, Geoffrey refers briefly to Merlin prophesying in Arthur's presence. He may have planned such a scene and even written it; but if so, he left it out of his final text and forgot to cancel the reference. It should be remembered that he wrote three books, and Merlin reappears in the third. However, some preliminary discussion is needed.

THE HISTORIA BRITTONUM

In the search for Merlin's origins, the most fruitful passage in the *History* is the one in which he makes his entry. Here we can be certain where Geoffrey found his material, and can take a confident step backward to a much earlier source. The first form of the confrontation with Vortigern occurs in a chaotic book called the *Historia Brittonum* (History of the Britons), which was compiled in Wales early in the ninth century. It is in poor Latin, far inferior both to classical style which precedes it and Geoffrey's which follows it. Some manuscripts name the compiler as Nennius, who worked at Bangor. The ascription is uncertain, but the book is often referred to as 'Nennius' and this is convenient. If the preface which gives his name is authentic, Nennius 'made one heap of all that he found', rummaging among old manuscripts and collecting traditions. The *Historia Brittonum* does give that impression, and its artlessness inspires a backhanded trust, not in its reliability as to fact, but in its freedom from Geoffrey's kind of invention. We can believe that its compiler has genuinely 'found' material and has not invented things. Indeed, he hardly seems capable of such invention. His materials may be a good deal older still, and some of them undoubtedly are.

Geoffrey's use of Nennius is obvious. His entire account of Vortigern is based upon one from Nennius, though of much less length and with much less detail. The episodes of the collapsing fortress, the intended sacrifice, and the young seer, the boy-without-a-father, all are here. The creatures in the pool are 'worms' or serpents – Geoffrey's dragons are a glorification of them – and the seer's interpretation is brief, portending an eventual British recovery, but not going on to an extended series of prophecies. The story ends with Vortigern making the lad overlord of western Britain and departing northwards.

However, there is one crucial difference. The lad is not called Merlin, but Ambrosius. Nennius identifies him with a fifth-century British leader, Ambrosius Aurelianus, who is known to history separately. He portrays this leader as showing prophetic gifts in his youth. In another passage, he speaks of Vortigern being afraid of him, and while the chronology is a hopeless muddle, it is implied that Ambrosius's youthful mantic display was a reason for the king's fear. Ambrosius is known in Welsh as Emrys Gwledig, and Nennius himself gives him that style. 'Emrys' is the Roman 'Ambrosius' in its Welsh form; and *gwledig* is a word originally applied to regional rulers, though it comes to mean 'prince' in a vaguer sense. The traditional scene of the incident, located by Geoffrey and Nennius only as in Snowdonia, is a hill-fort near Beddgelert called Dinas Emrys, or Ambrosius's Fort. Excavation has revealed traces of fifth-century inhabitants and even an ancient pool – though containing no dragons!

So Geoffrey's account of Merlin's début is re-telling and improving an older Welsh tale, but with a major change. The seer is *not* the youth who grew up to be the historical commander, Ambrosius or Emrys. Instead, Geoffrey calls him Merlin. Perhaps realising that readers familiar with Nennius may be aware of what he is doing, Geoffrey smooths over the difficulty by saying that Merlin was 'also called Ambrosius'. An easy way out, but it means he has to introduce another character called Ambrosius who *is* based upon the commander, too well-known a historical figure to be simply discarded. He transforms him into the rightful prince, Aurelius Ambrosius, and makes him king of Britain in succession to Vortigern. Mary Stewart, in her novel *The Crystal Cave*, offers a family relationship to render the doubling of Ambrosii more acceptable, but

Geoffrey himself does not. He leaves Merlin's alternative name hanging for a while, and then simply forgets it. He requires that his new character – the wonder-worker who prophesies a Celtic resurgence, sets up Stonehenge, and foretells and launches King Arthur – should definitely be Merlin, a distinct person.

Why make such a radical change? Where indeed does the new name come from? To find answers we must plunge into the past again by a different route.

THE ORIGIN OF MYRDDIN

In Geoffrey's Latin, 'Merlin' is *Merlinus*. This is a Latin form of a Welsh name, 'Myrddin'. Either Geoffrey himself, or some other writer who Latinised 'Myrddin', made it *Merlinus* and not *Merdinus*. After all, for readers in the Norman kingdom, *Merdinus* would have suggested the improper French word *merde*. Well before Geoffrey's time, the Welsh were telling stories about a Myrddin who was a prophet and perhaps also a poet. No verses credibly ascribed to him have survived, but there were poems that presented him as the speaker in dramatic monologues, to use Browning's term. The most important, *The Apple-Trees*, took the form of a lamentation for a disaster that had sent Myrddin wandering through the forest of Celidon, in southern Scotland. We will see what this disaster was in a moment.

When Geoffrey wrote his first book, *The Prophecies of Merlin*, he had this Myrddin in mind and fathered prophecies on him, while knowing almost nothing about him. When he wrote his second, *The History of the Kings of Britain*, he assumed – whether sincerely or as a literary device – that the young fifth-century seer, whom Nennius credited with similar gifts, was actually Myrddin. Geoffrey implied, without saying so, that Nennius's making him out to be Ambrosius Aurelianus was a mistake. But his own knowledge of Myrddin was still scanty. Consequently, he made a mistake himself. The disaster which Myrddin was depicted bewailing in *The Apple-Trees* was a real event: it was a tragic inter-British battle in Cumbria, but it was fought about 575, far too late. The youth who confounds Vortigern's magicians cannot, on the face of it, have been Myrddin. There is a gap of more than a century.

After writing his *History*, Geoffrey at last learned something tangible about the wandering prophet. He produced his third book, a long narrative poem entitled *The Life of Merlin*, adding the fatal battle and other events to what he had related already. In this poem, he opened up interesting new lines. Among other things, he gave Merlin a sister, Ganieda, who shared the prophetic inspiration. But his own self-inflicted crux proved too much. He tried to fudge the dates, the geography, and other details so as to make the fifth-century Merlin and the sixth-century Merlin a single person; but it could not be done. The story failed to cohere. An eminent Welsh author who came after him, Giraldus Cambrensis, realised this and concluded that there were two Merlins. Other Welshmen followed his lead. One of the summaries of bardic lore known as triads refers to a 'skilful bard' called Myrddin Emrys, i.e. Geoffrey's fifth-century Merlin Ambrosius, and another 'skilful bard' called Myrddin son of Morfryn, i.e. the sixth-century northerner. Of his father Morfryn, there is no significant record.

Before asking why Geoffrey created this problem, and why he identified the northern prophet with someone over a hundred years earlier, we must consider what more is known of the prophet. Regrettably, this involves bringing in still another name. 'Myrddin' is here a Welsh designation for a man elsewhere called Lailoken. As Lailoken, the prophet figures in the legendary '*Life*' of St Kentigern, the patron saint of Glasgow, and in two narratives related to it. He is said to have been guilty of stirring up strife that led to the Cumbrian battle. A heavenly voice denounced him for this misdeed, and told him that he must live out his days among the beasts of the wild. Looking up at the sky, he saw a horrifying vision of warriors brandishing fiery spears at him. Terrified, he fled half-mad into the forest of Celidon, cursed not only with exile but with the gift of second-sight. With his prophetic gift he foretold the death of a northern king, and made trouble for himself by revealing the infidelity of another king's wife. For himself, he predicted three different deaths, an apparent contradiction that caused amusement. But the adulterous queen incited her husband's shepherds to kill him. They gave him a beating and threw him from a height into the River Tweed, where his body was pierced by a stake. So he died in three ways: by blows, by impalement and by drowning. The exact nature of the three deaths varies a little between different versions.

This tale shows more clearly what the prophet's lamentation in *The Apple-Trees* is about. 'Myrddin' is simply a Welsh sobriquet for Lailoken, and the Myrddin of the poem is bewailing the woes which the story of Lailoken relates. There is no telling how much of the story of Lailoken is true, since the 'wild man of the woods', crazy yet inspired, is a recurrent folklore character. However, the Welsh give more details of the battle. It was recalled and mourned by the bards as 'futile', having been fought over a lark's nest. The phrase is a bitter joke, referring to Caerlaverock, the Fort of the Lark, a stronghold on the north side of the Solway Firth which was evidently a theme of contention. The battle took place in Arfderydd, now the parish of Arthuret (nothing to do with Arthur), in Cumbria near the Border. One of the chief leaders was Gwenddolau, and the precise location was close to his own stronghold, Caer Gwenddolau, another name that was corrupted and is now Carwinley. Myrddin, as the Welsh called him, fought on Gwenddolau's side. Their enemies were other Britons, some of them kinsmen, so that the battle had the special horror of civil war. The most important was King Rhydderch of Strathclyde, who appears also in the Lailoken matter. In the Welsh accounts, it is not so clear that Myrddin was actually to blame for the battle. But the slaughter was fearful, and his partial guilt caused him to be shunned and drove him into his forest wanderings half out of his mind, with sequels related in the stories calling him Lailoken.

Now, however, a firm distinction must be drawn, and this is the basis of the whole literary development. While Myrddin was indeed Lailoken, the Welsh saw more in him than the story-tellers of Scotland did. If they too had pictured him as a mere crazy soothsayer, Geoffrey would scarcely have thought him worth writing about. In his Welsh guise he was a more dignified, more tragic figure, and his gift had larger implications. Long before Geoffrey, he was quoted as a prophet on national issues in poems such as the *Armes Prydein* (*Omen of Britain*), probably composed about 930. This cited him as foretelling that the Celtic peoples would band together and triumph over the English.

Myrddin's reputed performance in this role was what Geoffrey had heard of first, so when he composed his series of 'prophecies', Merlin, his Latinised Myrddin, was the natural person to whom to ascribe them. Embedded in the mass of his own inventions there was certainly traditional matter, some of it genuinely connected with Myrddin – the most obvious instance being the prophecy of Celtic resurgence already quoted. In the *History of the Kings of Britain*, he tried to give Merlin with his prophecies a historical setting. At that stage he still knew nothing of the northerner's real story. In the prophecies, however, he had made Merlin foretell Arthur, on the assumption that he lived before Arthur, in the fifth century. His main source for that period was Nennius, and Nennius told of the boy-without-a-father who prophesied the Britons' recovery just as Myrddin had. It was enough of a hint. Geoffrey inferred, perhaps quite honestly, that the young seer *was* Myrddin and that the identification with Ambrosius was due to a confusion.

Later, when the truth dawned on him, he faced it. His poetic *Life of Merlin* shows that he did study the Myrddin–Lailoken materials. Even Merlin's surprising sister has an original in them. Geoffrey makes him more erudite, with an interest in astronomy and other sciences. But his efforts to equate two persons so far apart in time could not succeed. The Merlin whom he bequeathed to literature was an imperfect fusion of two characters; the first otherwise known as Ambrosius and belonging to the fifth century, the second otherwise known as Lailoken and belonging to the sixth. The first was more important for the Arthurian legend; the second supplied the name and is perhaps a little better supported by historical evidence.

Plainly, however, the inquiry cannot stop here, because of a remarkable fact – that both men did have names of their own. Geoffrey took 'Myrddin' and applied it, modified and Latinised, to someone already called Ambrosius. But before him the Welsh had taken 'Myrddin' and applied it to someone already called Lailoken. They themselves, using it as a sort of label, had supplied a justification for Geoffrey's attaching it to another person. What then did this shifting word 'Myrddin' signify?

Its etymology is odd. Geoffrey makes his character originate in south-west Wales. By implication, in the *History*, he adopts a claim that Carmarthen was named after him. The Welsh form of 'Carmarthen' is 'Caefyrddin', with a mutated consonant, 'City (of) Myrddin'. That makes the claim look plausible, but the truth is the other way about. The town's old name was *Moridunum*, the Sea-Fort, and 'Myrddin' is a Welsh version of it.

Here then we have a name or quasi-name rooted in south-west Wales, which is applied first to a late-sixth-century wild man of the woods with second sight, and then also to a supposed mid-fifth-century seer, though in the latter case it is applied by Geoffrey of Monmouth, who tries to persuade his readers that the two were the same. And that is as far as the consensus of scholarship goes. No one can be blamed for feeling it to be unsatisfactory. In effect, it makes the Merlin we know an artificial concoction by Geoffrey, and suggests that the only real original was an obscure northerner, mentally unbalanced, who lived much too late to do the things we associate with Merlin.

Anything beyond is admittedly conjectural. Yet one piece of evidence proves, at least, that the consensus of scholarship is not the whole story. If this evidence is to be given its due weight, it must be approached gradually. The starting-point is that curious name. Some have argued that the original Myrddin was neither Lailoken nor Ambrosius but a fictitious figure invented, when *Moridunum* was forgotten, to account for Caerfyrddin/Carmarthen. It is hard to see why anyone should have been identified with this phantasm. Lailoken, in particular, lived a long way from Carmarthen, and the early Welsh matter nowhere pretends that he had any links with it. The question arises, then, whether some local myth gave *Moridunum* or 'Myrddin' a deeper, more general significance, an overtone of prophetic inspiration. In that case, it could have been applied to the sixth-century wanderer on account of his second sight, irrespective of geography. Just possibly too, an awareness of it as a kind of prophetic title could have made it easier for Geoffrey to apply it to someone else.

An early 'Myrddin' item does furnish some support. In the Welsh poem-cycle *Gododdin*, composed by the bard Aneirin about 600, is a reference to the 'inspiration of Myrddin'. As to the date, this is inconclusive, because *Gododdin* suffered at the hands of interpolators. Yet even if the line is not by Aneirin, it hints at an association – still early – of 'Myrddin' with bardic prophecy, whoever the intended person, actual or mythical, may have been.

Perhaps a new line of country is opening up. Nikolai Tolstoy has given reason to think that there has to be more in this than a juggle with words. Even if we set aside Geoffrey's imaginings, it must be stressed again that the northern Myrddin alone is a greater figure than Lailoken as such is ever said to have been. As Myrddin he is more than a wilderness-dwelling madman. Poetic utterances are put in his mouth, he becomes a prophetic oracle for the Celtic peoples, and there are connotations of druidism, shamanism, and other venerable antecedents. I have discussed these topics, and their potential relevance, in *The Ancient Wisdom* and *Avalonian Quest*. By calling Lailoken 'Myrddin' the Welsh seem to have implied a significance in him which they believed they could discern, even if St. Kentigern's hagiographers could not.

Fortunately, we are far from exhausting the materials. To interpret Merlin more fully, we can pursue Geoffrey's account of him further. Not looking for history which is not there, but asking again where his ideas come from and why he portrays the character as he does. That inquiry points to a possible third figure who may supply a key to the two we already know. Also it leads to that stubborn item of evidence which the consensus of scholarship fails to handle. By a strange paradox, a further step in this complicated quest may be a path back towards simplicity, and the unification of characters who look so hopelessly separate.

MYRDDIN AND STONEHENGE

Geoffrey, it will be remembered, tells us that Merlin brought Stonehenge over from Ireland and set it up on Salisbury Plain. As an event in the fifth century, this is a far worse anachronism than the attempt to fuse characters a mere hundred-odd years apart. Stonehenge was formed in stages, mostly during the third millennium BC. The greater 'sarsen' stones were trundled over from the Marlborough Downs. But the smaller blue stones raise an intriguing issue. Some decades ago it was observed that they could not have come from anywhere near. The closest possible quarry was in the Preseli Mountains in south-west Wales, between Carn Meini and Foel Trigarn. Presumably that source had a special, irreplaceable sacredness. The blue stones were taken down to the sea and floated on rafts along the coast of South Wales, and then up some suitable river, doubtless the Bristol Avon, to a point requiring the minimum land haulage to the site. One or two geologists have disputed the need for such a remote origin, but Professor Colin Renfrew, in a BBC television programme on 9 June 1986, reaffirmed the Preseli explanation. It has long been urged – by Stuart Piggott and R. J. C. Atkinson, for instance – that in Geoffrey's narrative of stones brought by sea from the west, we have a remnant of a factual tradition handed down for thousands of years.

This view implies some kind of continuity linking the priests of the pre-Celtic era with the druids who followed them, and the bards who followed the druids. In the absence of writing, how else would the tradition have been handed down? But whether or not a specific story was transmitted, Geoffrey certainly has notions about the pre-Celtic megalith-builders. His name for Stonehenge, the Giants' Ring, shows its nature. Merlin tells the king that the stones have magical properties. Water poured over them cures the sick. Because of their healing virtue, giants conveyed them from Africa to Ireland in ancient times and put them up in the circular formation. Elsewhere in the *History*, Geoffrey speaks of giants in more general terms. He says they were the first inhabitants of Britain, then known as Albion, before the advent of the Trojans who were the original Britons. When the proto-Britons arrived, the giants were few and most of them were in Cornwall. Clearly these giants of his are the megalith-builders, imagined as huge because of the size of the stones, and Cornwall is the place where he has a concentration of them because of the number of Cornish megaliths. In other words, though he does not specifically discuss megaliths other than Stonehenge, mythical lore about them is present in his thoughts.

Stonehenge, however, does stand out, in actuality as well as in the *History of the Kings of Britain*. It is not simply a megalithic monument like the rest. It is a unique architectural structure, with its larger components artificially shaped by a vast amount of labour. Professor Renfrew maintains that towards 2000 BC an organised kingdom covered much of southern Britain, and that Stonehenge was its religious and political centre. There could well have been a myth of its being built on Salisbury Plain by a divine or semi-divine being, greater than the megalith-builders in general. If the transport of sea-borne stones from the west does imply an ancient tradition in Geoffrey's story, there is no reason to assume that this was the only thing the tradition mentioned. It could have said something of the being responsible. Does Geoffrey's Merlin embody a third figure, the creator and patron deity of Stonehenge, humanised, and transposed into the fifth century?

Suppose we imagine Stonehenge as Professor Renfrew's sacred centre. At such a place, major decisions would have been made, major decrees would have been proclaimed. If it was the creation and abode of a god, if perhaps its chief builder was a sacred king who incarnated him, a Greek parallel suggests that he may have had one aspect as a god of inspiration, like Apollo. Delphi was believed to be the centre or 'navel' of the earth. Apollo's oracle there played an influential part in the affairs of the Greek city-states, being, in fact, their sole bond of unity. Envoys from all of them, including Athens itself, consulted the Delphic oracle, not only on individual cases but on questions of policy. Sparta claimed that Apollo had dictated its constitution. In some of the cities Delphi had resident spokesmen who were attached to the government and interpreted the god's messages. Plato, in his *Republic*, advises that 'the greatest and finest and most important of legislative acts' – those establishing religion – should be determined by Apollo through Delphi: 'For he is the national expositor who explains these things to all men from his seat at the navel of the earth.' We might picture something of the kind at Stonehenge, with a presiding god who guided rulers' decisions: a god, therefore, of inspiration like Apollo, speaking through royal omens or the ecstatic prophecy of shamans, ancestors of the druids.

All this would be fairly pointless guesswork if it were not that such a conception might unravel the entire Merlin problem. The reemergence in Geoffrey's *History* of the presiding genius of Stonehenge, designated as Merlin or Myrddin, suggests a solution. If 'Myrddin' denoted this being, and he was a god of inspiration, 'Myrddin' would have carried that notion and might have been attached, as a sort of honorific, to any appropriately inspired person. Greece had another god of inspiration differing from Apollo but also associated with Delphi, Dionysus, otherwise known as Bacchus. An ecstatic votary under his control, a 'Bacchos', was more or less identified with the god. The name 'Myrddin' in the Welsh matter goes with pronouncements on major national issues. It could be that the chief royal builder of Stonehenge, and the fifth-century seer credited with predicting Vortigern's doom, and the sixth-century wanderer said to have foretold a Celtic resurgence, were all linked or capable of being linked as mortal vessels of an immortal Myrddin, under the same inspiration. The prehistoric god would, of course, have been called so by the Welsh in retrospect, somewhat as eighteenth-century English poets referred to the gods of Homer by Roman names; 'Jupiter' meaning the god actually called Zeus, 'Juno' meaning Hera, and so on. These hypothetical Myrddins may have been only three in a long succession, but if they were the three of whom Geoffrey had some inkling, we can see what he may have done. Lacking the key, he tried unsuccessfully to unite them by making them the same person.

On this showing, his attaching the designation to the fifth-century character was certainly a mistake, in the sense that the Welsh matter concerning Myrddin referred to the later figure. Yet it could have been a felicitous guess, or it could have reflected actual knowledge after all, and a hazy awareness of what *Gododdin* calls 'the inspiration of Myrddin' without an understanding of its full implications.

Geoffrey's allusion to Merlin's familiar spirit is interesting. The two Myrddins depicted as living in the fifth and sixth centuries belong to a nominally Christian Britain, and would have been Christians themselves after their fashion. Yet enough paganism lingered to allow their inspiration a semi-pagan quality. The god, however, would have been downgraded into what Geoffrey makes Merlin speak of, a familiar spirit.

Is the god pure fantasy? Not quite. One occurrence of 'Myrddin' has caused perplexity by its refusal to fit, and this is the point where the consensus of scholarship has nothing to offer. There is a Welsh manuscript called the *White Book of Rhydderch*. Among much else, it contains a myth that went into the making of the tale of the fighting dragons. This book, with support from other manuscripts, includes a text entitled *The Names of the Island of Britain*. The title is taken from the opening paragraph. Rachel Bromwich maintains that the material in it is much older than Geoffrey and preserves traditional ideas about early Britain which he suppressed in his own work:

'The first name that this island bore, before it was taken or settled: Myrddin's Precinct. And after it was taken and settled, the Island of Honey. And after it was conquered by Prydein son of Aedd the Great it was called the Island of Prydein (Britain).'

'Island of Honey' is peculiar, as, according to Dr Bromwich, is the form of the Welsh itself *Y Vel Ynys*. She remarks that the normal form would be *Ynys Vel*, and suggests (surely rightly) that the name originated in a corruption of *Ynys Veli*, meaning the Island of Beli – Beli being a mythical king of ancient Britain who is well attested in Welsh literature. But, of course, 'Myrddin's Precinct', Britain's name 'before it was taken or settled', is the remarkable phrase. Since the island could hardly have been called 'Myrddin's Precinct' before it had *any* inhabitants, the allusion may be to a time before the settlement that Welsh legend counted. At any rate, this Myrddin is manifestly prehistoric.

Rachel Bromwich confesses that 'it is difficult to account for the association of the name of *Myrddin* with this tradition'. Indeed it is. No one could have supposed that thousands of years ago, the island was called by a name derived from the Myrddin of the sixth century. The sentence implies that the sixth-century Myrddin's designation was related to something vastly older, to the myth or cult of a being whom it was proper to call 'Myrddin' likewise. He could have been a god, a divine ruler or guardian of the island. He might have been regarded as such because he was the patron and inspirer of its sacred centre Stonehenge, the focus of its life, according to Professor Renfrew.

Why should British Celts, looking back to a pre-Celtic deity, have retroactively named him Myrddin – He-of-Moridunum? The natural answer is that he was connected with the place, having one of his cultic dwellings or shrines in that area. A glance at the map of Wales is helpful. Carmarthen, or Moridunum, is the chief inhabited centre in the very part of Wales from which Stonehenge's blue stones were brought, less than twenty miles from the quarry in the Preseli Mountains. Merlin, who conveys the stones by sea from the west, could have begun as a god with a cultic dwelling in that part of Wales, whose people conveyed the blue stones from that region. They may have made the colossal effort in the belief that the sacred centre of the land, Stonehenge, would be valid only if it included stones from an area that belonged specially to this god, the source of public inspiration. When the tradition of the feat was handed down to the Celtic Britons, the divine presence at Stonehenge was He-of-Moridunum, Myrddin, finally humanised and Latinised as Merlin.

Let us, then, indulge the notion that in a distant past, the Carmarthen god was tutelary deity of the land, which was therefore his 'precinct'. He may have had many functions, as had Apollo; but as a god of inspiration he spoke to his people at their sacred centre Stonehenge, like Apollo speaking to the Greeks at their own sacred centre Delphi. Or perhaps his oracular shrine, his Delphi, was in the Carmarthen area itself, and Stonehenge was the place where his messages were published, and decrees were proclaimed in accordance with them. A tradition of his deity was transmitted by priests or story-tellers to his people's Celtic successors, and kept alive by druids and bards. He was given a Celtic name or epithet taken from Carmarthen, from the site of the temple which the tradition spoke of. There was a thread of continuity, and persons delivering mantic utterances on public issues were deemed to be his mouthpieces or guises and given the divine epithet – thus becoming Myrddin's-men or simply Myrddins, whether they were named Ambrosius or Lailoken or anything else. In the *Gododdin* line, this perhaps underlies the poet's reference to 'the inspiration of Myrddin'. Another poet employs 'Myrddin' almost synonymously with *awen* 'the muse', not in the personified female sense, but as the power incarnate in the inspired bard. Geoffrey of Monmouth, after centuries of Christianity, no longer understands. Vaguely aware of a plurality of Myrddins, and of a bond among them, he can only unite the characters whom he presents as Myrddin by the fancy that the builder of Stonehenge on Salisbury Plain, and the fifth-century seer, and the sixth-century wanderer, were identical.

We catch a glimpse of such an awareness in an even later author, who offers another would-be solution. The Welsh triad about the skilful bards, already cited, mentions Myrddin Emrys (i.e. the 'Ambrosius' Merlin) and Myrddin son of Morfryn (i.e. the 'Lailoken' Merlin), and adds the famous bard Taliesin, another vessel of inspiration. The triad's composer knows them to be three individuals. Yet a sixteenth-century Welsh chronicler named Elis Gruffudd, the preserver of much legendary lore about Taliesin, is conscious of a deeper connection than a shared skill. He claims that Myrddin Emrys was actually reincarnated as Taliesin, and then as Myrddin son of Morfryn. An obvious objection is that the second and third of the trio were alive at the same time. Geoffrey, in his *Life of Merlin*, has a meeting between them. But the point is that Elis Gruffudd senses a profound unity. Unable to follow Geoffrey in making out the three to have been the same person in the usual sense, he unites them by metempsychosis.

As to the hypothetical god, no trustworthy evidence will take us back as far as Stonehenge. The monument's orientation suggests a solar cult, but this is a false clue as regards Apollo or an Apollo-like deity; Apollo was *not* originally a sun-god. However, in the fourth century BC, Hecataeus of Abdera does testify to a god in Britain whom he describes as its chief deity and identifies with Apollo, speaking of him as a musician, as Apollo was. His often-quoted passage includes a reference to a calendric scheme hinting at druid information, and also mentions a 'notable round temple', which seems (the text is not quite unequivocal) to be dedicated to the British Apollo. Many who have discussed this passage have claimed that the temple is Stonehenge, and it would be gratifying if it were. Unfortunately, the Greek word means 'spherical', not 'circular'. If the reading is correct, the temple can hardly be anything but a myth, since the Britons certainly constructed no spherical buildings. A slight emendation would allow it to be 'spiral', recalling Apollo's association with spiral dances and designs representing the Cretan labyrinth. (I have gone into that topic in *Avalonian Quest*; to pursue it here would be to stray too far from Merlin.) What matters is that while Hecataeus's round temple may be another false clue, he proves that the British Celts had a god identifiable with Apollo, whether or not his origins were pre-Celtic.

A BRITISH APOLLO

Inscriptions of the second and third centuries AD show that the recognised British Apollo then was a god known as Maponos. He was the 'divine youth', patron of music and poetry, and hence of inspiration, at least in one sense. The inscriptions are in Lancashire, Cumbria and Northumberland, and suggest that Maponos was popular in the zone of Hadrian's Wall. A seventh-century geographical text, the Ravenna Cosmography, mentions a *locus* or 'place' of Maponos which was apparently a northern cult-centre, and may have been one or other of two places where a form of 'Maponos' survives, Lochmaben in Dumfries-shire, and Clochmabenstane, a megalith by the Solway Firth near Gretna. Since traces of the god's cult are detectable in Gaul, there is no reason why it should not have been known in southern as well as northern Britain. Hecataeus, though writing some centuries before the inscriptions, may quite well mean Maponos when he talks about a British Apollo.

Like some other characters in the Celtic pantheon, Maponos re-surfaces in Welsh legend. He becomes Mabon ap Modron (Mabon son of Modron). The latter is also a Celtic divinity, the goddess Matrona, tutelary power of the River Marne in Gaul. Her son appears in the *Mabinogion* tale *Culhwch and Olwen*, and, further disguised, in Arthurian romances. The curious thing about the name 'Mabon ap Modron' is that it means 'Son, son of Mother', and looks like another case of a designation or epithet rather than a name. Furthermore, this is a most unusual way of referring to a male person. Welsh would normally use a patronymic and name the father. Matronymics are not totally unknown, but 'Mabon ap Modron' is hardly even that.

Figure 2   Mabon, the Celtic Apollo

Maponos, or Mabon, has a mother who is simply 'mother' and no adequately attested father at all. Rachel Bromwich cites a Welsh text in which *Mabon* is used to mean Christ, who had no earthly father. But the more significant echo here is of the fifth-century Merlin, Myrddin Emrys, the boy-without-a-father. Too little is known of these matters to allow the parallel to be pressed, but it exists. The peculiarity of the fatherless seer, Myrddin Emrys, is the same as that of the fatherless British Apollo, who, as a god of inspiration, *could* be the original divine Myrddin.

CLUES FROM THE CARMARTHEN AREA

To take these possibilities further would require proof of a cult in the Carmarthen area. Archaeology offers nothing persuasive. Some Merlin folklore may be merely a product of the medieval legend. A tree called the Priory Oak, which used to stand near the centre of Carmarthen, certainly was. It was also known as Myrddin's Tree, and a popular rhyme declared:

'When Myrddin's Tree shall tumble down,
Then shall fall Carmarthen Town.'

Civic authorities tried to avert this disaster by bracing the tree with iron supports. Eventually it was removed, and nothing can be seen now but a sliver of its wood in the museum.

A shade more interesting is Bryn Myrddin or Merlin's Hill. This is two-and-a-half miles east, up the valley of the River Tywi. There is no evident reason why a hill at some distance from the town should have attracted the legend, unless there were a well-established tradition about it. Local lore speaks of Merlin's Cave, a hidden chamber under the hill where he is imprisoned, and his voice can be heard below the ground.

Edmund Spenser, in *The Faerie Queene*, gives a different account of the cave. He locates it in the grounds of Dynevor Castle near Llandeilo, quite a long way up the river, far enough to suggest an independent story, not due solely to the later associations of

Carmarthen itself. Merlin, he says, was in the habit of retiring into the cave to commune with spirits.

> 'There the wise Merlin whilom wont (they say)
> To make his wonne [dwelling] low underneath the ground,
> In a deep delve, far from the view of day,
> That of no living wight he might be found,
> When so he counselled with his sprites encompassed round.'

Spenser gives some advice to the sight-seer:

> 'And if thou ever happen that same way
> To travel, go to see that dreadful place:
> It is an hideous hollow cave (they say)
> Under a rock that lies a little space
> From the swift Barry, tumbling down apace,
> Amongst the woody hills of Dynevowre;
> But dare thou not, I charge, in any case,
> To enter into that same baleful bower,
> For fear the cruel fiends should thee unwares devour.'

He adds that if you listen from the outside, you can hear weird noises issuing from beneath the rock.

Spenser weakens his credibility slightly by wrongly naming the river. Yet surely this is a striking description? He has not taken it from any recognised Merlin legend, and it has just a hint of the oracular caverns of classical antiquity. Apollo's Italian oracle at Cumae, to judge from Virgil, was an intimidating cave-sanctuary where the Sibyl was possessed by the god.

A Greek architect named Trophonius, reputed builder or part-builder of the temple at Delphi, was awarded posthumous semi-divine status and an oracle of his own. This too was in a cave. Pilgrims supposedly entered the infernal regions, and the experience was so awe-inspiring that they lost the power to smile, temporarily or, according to some accounts, permanently. A suppliant under-went days of preliminary purification by bathing and eating sacred food. When the time for the visit came, he drank spring-water that prepared his memory for the ordeal, threaded a labyrinthine arrangement of spikes and railings, descended a ladder into a chasm, and was dragged though a cleft into subterranean darkness. An unseen assailant struck him a blow on the head, and an unseen speaker revealed the future and other mysteries. He was then hauled up again and questioned, still in a daze, as to what he had heard. The invisible speaker was supposed to be instructed in what to say by the ghost of Trophonius himself, dwelling in the underworld in the form of a serpent. Conceivably, Spenser had heard some immemorial Welsh tradition of such a place, a frightening oracular cave of the Britons' god of inspiration, He-of-Moridunum, Myrddin.

MERLIN IN LATER HISTORY

Aside from all speculation, the course taken by medieval Arthurian literature is impressive in itself. It was the Merlin of Geoffrey's *History*, the fifth-century seer, whom the romancers adopted and who became the Merlin we know. Whatever the enhancements drawn from a Stonehenge-builder and a sixth-century prophet, they were firm as to the primary manifestation. The reason was simple. They wanted to pursue an alluring possibility, which Geoffrey himself had strangely neglected: that Merlin not only foretold Arthur, and masterminded his birth, but lived on afterwards as his counsellor and magical helper. To do these things he and no one else had to be the character in the *History*. The result was fascinating. Something like an indwelling godhead reappeared in greater strength. It seems to have been there, latently, all the time. The Merlin of the developed legend grew into the tutelary power of Britain, fostering a golden age.

His career in this role, as we can trace it in many tales and poems, incorporates the career assigned to him in the *History*, but is far grander and also ambiguous. The traditions that have moulded it show him to be a transitional figure, with a footing in two worlds. He conforms after his fashion to a Christian society, yet he is a sort of druid. Someone like this, who, as it were, has it both ways, belongs in the context and atmosphere of early Celtic Christianity, which often domesticated the old gods and myths rather than anathematising them, as is clear in the *Mabinogion* and elsewhere. Medieval Christendom took a more black-and-white view of things, yet the Merlin of its romancers bears, distorted, the stamp of his origins.

Unable to admit his begetting by a spirit merely neutral and mysterious, they assert that his non-human father was one of the host of hell trying to create an anti-Christian prophet. The devil's intention, they explain, was thwarted by the piety of his female victim, so that her son Merlin had superhuman powers but was willing to employ them for good ends. The contrivance is ingenious yet awkward, an attempt to fit him into a rigid good-and-evil scheme to which he is senior.

Armed with his oddly-derived powers, Merlin denounces the usurper Vortigern and foretells his doom. In this episode, the chief point to notice is his age. He is still definitely a boy and indeed a child prodigy. If we consider subsequent events and the time they cover, in Geoffrey himself and in any of the romantic developments, we see that the modern semi-comic image of Merlin as an old man with a long white beard is completely bogus. It may not go further back than Tennyson, and it is plainly incompatible with Geoffrey and the romancers. Merlin is young for a large part of the story (we might almost dare to recall the 'divine youth', the British Apollo) and unlikely to be past his forties when he drops out. He is vigorous, brilliant, active, not a mere doddering accessory of the court, even at the end.

Of his superhuman feat in transplanting Stonehenge, little need be added. What he creates in so doing, in the context of his expanded role, is a national shrine hallowed by the bodies of Britain's nobles and kings. When he organises the conception of Arthur, he is not simply doing a trick to oblige Uther, he is bringing about the advent of a kind of Messiah. He takes the wonderful child away to be fostered out of sight and danger, until the time comes for his epiphany. He then arranges the magical test of the Sword in the Stone to prove Arthur's title when he emerges, marking him off from the ordinary mortals, whom the test defeats. Once Arthur is securely enthroned, Merlin uses his gifts in the King's cause, giving him confidential glimpses of the way things will go.

Arthur wields the sword drawn from the stone till he breaks it in combat. Thereupon, Merlin conducts him to meet the Lady of the Lake – herself a divine or semi-divine being out of pagan antiquity – and obtains the more marvellous Excalibur for him, together with its scabbard, which prevents him from losing blood when wounded.

Through Merlin, also, the Round Table becomes a mystical object. In Geoffrey's *History*, Arthur founds his order of knighthood, but nothing is said about any item of furniture. The Table makes its entry in a French poetical version of the *History* by Wace, who claims that it was a feature of the Arthurian story as told by the Bretons. But his explanation for it is strictly practical – that Arthur wanted to avoid disputes over relative importance which a long table would encourage. In romance, however, the Table is constructed under Merlin's direction and given religious and cosmic bearings. It is a replica of a table which Joseph of Arimathea fashioned for the Grail. This in turn imitated the table of the Last Supper, becoming the third successive table symbolising the Trinity, and linking spiritual and chivalric ideals. The Round Table of Arthur corresponds to the world of earthly life, and its shape has a further meaning, in representing the round world and heavens. But its link with its predecessor is kept always in view by its reserving an empty place – the Perilous Seat, destined for the knight who will achieve the Grail. While Merlin is no longer present when the Grail Quest is undertaken, he has prepared the way for that too, and for the kingdom's reunion with its hidden spiritual treasure.

So important does Merlin grow that Arthur's Britain is practically Myrddin's Precinct over again, the realm of the god restored. This is a mythification like the mythification of Arthur himself. If, as is likely, the Arthur of legend is based upon a real fifth-century king, could the same be inferred about Merlin? Was there after all a fifth-century figure whom we may call Merlin Ambrosius, Myrddin Emrys, as well as the Myrddin of the sixth century?

The utmost guess that can be offered honestly is that a man did exist who disturbed Vortigern, befriended his successors, and was reputed to be inspired. While there is no tangible evidence for him, the question is open. Obviously, romancers and novelists who have depicted Merlin in their stories are inventing. However, it cannot be stated dogmatically that they are inventing out of nothing at all.

Figure 3   Merlin and the Thirteen Treasures of Britain

There may have been a person of the right sort at the right time. A real 'original Merlin' in the company of a real 'original Arthur', probably during the second half of the fifth century, is a possibility allowed by current appraisal of the period. On that possibility, imagination may fairly work, so long as it is clearly accepted that history can make no pronouncement.

However, to revert to the Merlin of the expanded legend. He fades from the scene long before Arthur – quite early in the reign, in Malory's version. His downfall comes through the strange episode of Nimue, or Viviane, in which his wisdom fails. He knows he is set on a fatal course, yet can do nothing to save himself. His passionate desire for the lake-damsel, and their long journeying together, prove him again to be very far from decrepitude. When she has entrapped him in a magical prison, the realm he has created endures for a long time, till its inherent human flaws destroy it. But what happens to Merlin? Like Arthur, he has an alleged grave, two or three in fact, where Arthur has only one. Yet we are never told how he escaped from the cave (or whatever it was) in which his lady immured him, as he would have had to do in order to die elsewhere and be buried.

Perhaps the familiar tale is a medieval anti-feminist fantasy. It would be pleasant to believe in a more authentic tradition, in which Merlin resembles Arthur as an immortal. Such a tradition may survive in a Welsh story which asserts that he is living in an invisible house of glass on Bardsey Island (Ynys Enelli), by his own choice, not imprisoned. He has nine companions with him, and is custodian of the Thirteen Treasures of the Island of Britain, wonder-working objects concealed from the Saxons and other conquerors. He also has the true throne of the British realm, on which he will enthrone Arthur when the King returns. Some say he is asleep, like Arthur in his cave. Others deny it.

If I am right, we need not dismiss this tradition as a fairy-tale about a particular man who may or may not have lived, centuries ago. It symbolises a lasting faith. The spirit once ascribed to the god, the spirit that produced Merlin and was embodied in him, has never perished. Because it can embody itself again, the succession may not be ended – another Merlin may arise.

Merlyns Tweyne

At Nemyn in Norþ Wales
A litel ilond þere is,
Þat hatte Bardeseie;
Monkes woneþ þere alweie.
Men lyueþ so longe in þat hurste,
Þat þe eldest deiȝep furst.
Me seiþ þat Merlyn i-buried þere is,
Þat hiȝte also Siluestris.
There were Merlyns tweyne
And prophecied alle beyne.
Oon hiȝte Ambrose and Merlyn,
And wes i-gete of gobolyn.
In Demecia at Caermerthyn,
Vnder kyng Fortigeryn,
He tolde oute his prophecie;
Euene in Snawdonye.
At þe heed of þe water of Conewy,
In þe side of mount Eryry,
Dynays Embreys a Walsche,
Ambrose his hille on Englisch,
Kyng Fortigern sat on
Þe water side, and was wel ful of woon.
Þan Ambrose Merlyn prophecied so
To fore hym þere riȝt þoo.
What wight wolde wene
Þat a fend myȝt now gete a childe?
Som men wolde mene.
Þat he may no werk soche wilde.
That fend þat gooþ a nyȝt,
Wommen wel ofte to begile,
Incubus haue be ryȝt:

47

And gileþ men oþer while.
Succubus is þat wight
God graunte vs non suche vile
Who þat in hir myȝt
Comeþ wonder hap schal smyle.
Wiþ wonder dede
Boþe men and wommen sede
Fendes wyl kepe
Wiþ craft, and brynge in on hepe.
So fendes wilde
May make wommen bere childe;
Ȝit neuere in mynde
Was childe of fendes kynde.
For wiþ oute eye
There myȝte childe non suche deye.
Clergie makeþ mynde
Deeþ sleeþ nouȝt fendes kynde;
But deth slowe Merlyn,
Merlyn was ergo no gobelyn.
[R.] Anoþer Merlin of Albalonde,
Þat now hatte Scottelonde,
Hadde names two,
Siluestris and Calidonius also,
Of þat wode Calidonie,
For þere he tolde his prophecie;
And heet Siluestris as wel,
For whan he was in [a] batel,
And sigh aboue a grisliche kynde,
And fil anon out of his mynde;
And made no more bood,
But ran to þe wood.
Siluestris is wood,
Other wilde of mood;
Other elles,
Þat at þe wode he dwelles.
R. Siluestris Merlyn
Tolde prophecie wel and fyn,
And prophecied ful sure
Vnder kyng Arthure
Openliche, nouȝt so cloos

48

As Merlyn Ambros.
There beeþ hilles in Snowdowye,
Þat beeþ wonderliche hiȝe,
Wiþ heiȝte as grete way
As a man may goo a day;
And hiȝte Eryry in Walische,
Snowy hilles on Englische.
In þese hilles þere is
Leese i-now for al Walis;
Þis hil in þe cop berys
Tweye grete fische werys,
Conteyned in þe oon pond;
Meueþ wiþ the wynd an ilond,
As þeigh he dede swymme,
And neiȝeth to þe brymme;
So þat herdes haueþ greet wonder
And weneþ þat þe world meueþ vnder.

Polychronicon Ranulphi Higden (14th C).
translated by John Trevisa, 1587

PART 2
THE ARCHETYPE OF MERLIN

Introduction

by R. J. Stewart

In Gareth Knight's essay on the archetype of Merlin, and in the two short papers which follow, many of the essential aspects of the figure of Merlin *as a magician* are brought right into the present day. This direct application of imagery, poetry, and archetypical symbolism within modern society is typical of genuine magic. Although historical and cultural sources are vital for continuity and for an overview that keeps us from assuming that we are the only truly developed civilisation, magic is made by applying images to immediate matters such as good, evil, and living human relationships. This is no trite statement, for as Dr Knight observes, the apparently fictitious symbols of corruption are utterly manifest today in actual events, or more terrifyingly, in potential disasters of a global nature.

We may see Merlin as an allegorical figure, as an archetype, or as a source of inspiration; but none of these are of any value unless he is also defined within an utterly modern context. In this chapter, we read of blue stones, wizards' robes, magical seduction, and various ancient poems and texts; but we also hear of 'star wars' technology, the vanity of materialist space research and exploration in a world of starvation and misery, under the threat of nuclear war. The repeated message, if we choose to define it in such a manner, is that truth is found at home, in our hearts and in the heart of the planet. Merlin clearly demonstrates this in all of his aspects and adventures.

Just as the apparently fictitious symbols of corruption are made manifest, so superficially outdated symbols of regeneration and transformation may be made effective as a counterbalance. Merlin, Arthur, the UnderWorld, and the vast panoply of ancient magical and spiritual traditions, are based upon realities within human consciousness; thus they may never be 'outdated', even though the vehicles of expression (such as texts, books, cards, films) are in need of revision and re-assessment. Ultimately, the true vehicle of expression for spiritual truth is the human being; just as we are so bitterly and obviously the vehicles for material degradation and self-destructive folly.

Dr Knight advises us constantly that Merlin is a steward or holder of power: the source of that power is the same as the source of the stars; it is universal Being ... a fact that cannot be denied even on an atheistic level, for all power comes from a universe of energy and entropy. Power itself, however, is neutral; it is will or lack of will that defines a polarisation of power towards good or evil effect. In social terms, this means responsibility to fellow humans and to the generations yet unborn; for despite Merlin's supernatural origins as half-human, half-spirit, or daemon, he instigated a number of ethical and social patterns, according to the traditions of the court of Arthur, and left a lengthy set of previsions to advise the people of future times regarding corruption, hatred, folly, greed, and certain key images of transformation which purify these imbalances. These previsions are found in *The Prophecies of Merlin*.

At the close of his main essay, Dr Knight reminds us that Merlin is an ambassador from another world. This is not meant in the science-fiction sense, but in the sense of an archetype of energies and modes of consciousness which are barely being rediscovered by modern research in science, though they have been known and taught for thousands of years, often in an incoherent manner, within active esoteric traditions. Once again, it must be stressed that Merlin is not part of the fashionable trend for 'the occult', but instead is a figure from a demanding ethical poetical tradition of magical maturity; a tradition in which the imagination is purified and directed towards specific ends, rather than allowed to run riot with grandiose visions of domination, or to fester within the ludicrous confines of debased commercial occultism. Here, then, is Gareth Knight's presentation of 'The Archetype of Merlin'.

The Archetype of Merlin

by Gareth Knight

The word 'archetype' comes from two Greek words: *arche* meaning beginning; and *tupos* meaning figure or image. An archetype is therefore the original pattern of a thing, or the model from which it is made. Bob Stewart has defined it as a key image, which gives shape and direction to energies arising out of the primal source of all being. What we are looking for is the original pattern, or the prime model, the key image of Merlin.

To the popular imagination, Merlin is a magician. To the childish imagination, arguably the truest and purest form of the imagination we have, Merlin is a bearded man in a tall pointed hat and long cloak, dark in colour with stars upon it. He probably carries a magic wand with which, amongst other things, he is able to perform dazzling feats of pyrotechnics – an old man in a funny dress who can make fireworks. He is also perhaps a little irascible, but then people in charge of fireworks often are short tempered, because although fireworks are very attractive, exciting looking things, they can be very dangerous if one does not know what one is doing. Perhaps this idea accounts for the related tradition of the magician's apprentice, who by venturing to dabble with things beyond his knowledge and capability, brings considerable difficulties upon himself, and sometimes upon his master, who has to sort out the trouble.

From this childish image, much that is of value can be gleaned. We see that Merlin, by his long flowing beard, is an old man, signifying great wisdom and experience. The fact of his unusual dress tells us that he is not, to say the least, a conventional type of person. His mastery of pyrotechnics indicates that he is in command of forces that are of a spectacular beauty needing skilled and careful handling. In the shape of his hat, which is long and pointed, there is a hint of associations with witches and their traditional lore. The tall hat is also a part of the national costume of Wales, also worn by women, which gives another dimension to Merlin's associations and antecedents. A man from the far West dressed in traditional headgear usually seen only on women. Is there also a link with the timeless traditions of men dressing up as women in certain ancient forms of ritual dance? Finally, the symbols on his cloak and hat indicate a strong association with the stars and other heavenly bodies. Summarising all this, we have a being of great wisdom and great proficiency in the fields of traditional, fiery and stellar lore.

Traditional lore pertains to our ancestry, history, tribal and national and racial heritage: it is the destiny imposed upon us by land and blood. Fiery lore is by nature a medium of transformation, which can be rapid and radical. Fire itself, like the light and heat of the sun, is the source of matter and life. Starry lore pertains to matters far beyond the limits of our earthly, planetary existence, and beyond the natural existential limits of our human condition.

Merlin is thus no ordinary wiseman or wizard writ large, as we discover when we turn to the early literature such as Geoffrey of Monmouth's *History of the Kings of Britain*, which contains within it a more ancient oral tradition. Here we read that Merlin is a very different character and creature from the professional wizards in the court of King Vortigern.

Vortigern himself is not only a usurper to his throne in North Wales, he is also a quisling; in order to help defend himself against his fellow kinsmen, the Pendragon line of Celtic kings, he invites the heathen Saxons into the land as professional mercenaries. Before he knows where he is, he also has problems with these foreign hirelings. He then attempts to build a powerful tower of strength upon the site of the ancient holy city of Dinas Emrys on Snowdon, only to find that it will not stand, and so he goes to his permanent staff of magicians, to ascertain the reason, and to seek a remedy.

The magicians are not in a position to discern the real cause of the trouble, steeped as they are in the self-same delusions, guilty aspirations and physical and political power-based assumptions as the usurper king. But the solution they propose is one that comes from the depths, not to say dregs, of the past: the sacrifice of the innocent – a custom and practice of which the evidence is to be found, in the form of skeletal remains, under foundation stones and door steps of houses, and under ancient bridges across certain rivers. Generally, the sacrifices are set as guardians of the way, from one state or condition of existence to another: across a river boundary, or from out doors to within.

The innocent have a particularly potent effect in this grim and bizarre technology of primitive magic, but in this case, the most easily available innocent victim, a child, is not enough. An especial category of child is required: one that was not born of human father.

What kind of child has no human father? The idea comes from an old tradition commonplace in the ancient world: that of the divine king, whose parentage should be that of the gods.

Vortigern and his magicians were usurpers to a man, in all likelihood attempting to find some ritually chosen child-king from another tribe to sacrifice; so that his blood, mixed with the mortar of the foundation stones, would enable their dark tower to stand.

However, they had not reckoned on a superior magic, power and authority to their own nor that Merlin would be a wielder of this higher magic, and a bearer of this superior power and authority.

Young as Merlin was, he could see through Vortigern's plan and motives, and he also saw the hidden reasons for the perpetual downfall of the tower. Having revealed the true reasons and confounded the magicians of Vortigern, the young Merlin then proceeded to prophecy concerning the future of the nation and the world.

We need not go into the details of his prophecies; they will no doubt be taken up by Bob Stewart, who has written a book on the subject. But they serve to make the main point that Merlin is not just a magician. Anyone can become a magician: there are even correspondence courses for it nowadays. He was a superior being, bearing insights into time, and into wider perspectives of human affairs, than any of his contemporaries. This constitutes a fundamental part and basis of the archetype of Merlin.

Cited in the Bible, in the thirteenth chapter of the book of Genesis, and in the Epistle to the Hebrews, we find the prototype of a being 'without father, without mother, without descent', who aided and assisted the patriarch Abraham in his battles with the Kings of

Edom, just as Merlin aided Arthur in his battles with the ancient kings who sought to deny him his birthright. This biblical figure was named Melchizedek. The name derives from two words: *melech* – a king, and *zadok* – a priest, and signifies priest-king. The kingdom, however, is not necessarily of this world; indeed Melchizedek is described as King of Salem, which translated means 'King of Peace' – not a state easily found in this world.

THE STORY OF MERLIN

It will repay us to look in more detail at the circumstances of Merlin's birth and his early prowess. These are described in *The History of the Kings of Britain* by Geoffrey of Monmouth, written in Latin and completed about 1135. The book proved to be a bestseller, and is still on sale, in translation, in paperback in all good bookshops today. It was also translated into Norman-French, by a Channel Island monk called Wace, in about 1150, and later into Old English by the Anglo-Saxon Layamon, in about 1190.

I would like to refer to Layamon's Old English account, rather than to the earlier Latin and Norman-French versions of Geoffrey or Wace. I use this account because, as an intensely Engish poet, he is closer to most of us and even translating the Old English alliterative verse into modern speech, there is a beat about it that brings a breath of fresh air from the ancient shires that is lost in the Latin and the French.

Layamon also expands upon his originals, and gives us a fuller account of things, drawing from the native folk traditions assimilated by the early English – who were not at constant loggerheads with the Celts as is often assumed; there was a considerable degree of assimilation. This is evidence indeed of how the land claims an incoming people as its own. In Layamon, we find that the English are also looking forward to the return of Arthur, although recognising that he has a special relationship with the British, as one of their native heroes. This occurs at the end of the book, where we have the first written account of Arthur being carried away by maidens in a boat to Avalon. This does not appear in Geoffrey or Wace. There is, moreover, a special relationship with elves – a point we shall return to later.

The wounded Arthur speaks:

' "And I will fare to Avalun,   to the fairest of all maidens,
to Argante the queen,   an elf most fair
and she shall make   my wounds all sound;
make me all whole   with healing draughts.

And afterwards I will come again to   and dwell with the Britons in
     my kingdom,   mickle joy."

Even with the words   there approached from the sea
that was a short boat,   floating with the waves;
and two women therein,   wondrously formed;
and they took Arthur anon,   and bare him quickly,
and laid him softly down,   and forth they gan depart.

Then it was accomplished   that Merlin once had said
that mickle care should be   of Arthur's departure.

The Britons believe yet   that he is alive,
and dwelleth in Avalun   with the fairest of all elves;
and the Britons ever yet expect   when Arthur shall return.

Was never the man born,   or ever any lady chosen,
that knoweth of the truth,   to say more of Arthur.

But once was a sage hight Merlin;   he said with words –
his sayings were true   that an Arthur should yet come
     to help the English'.

But to return to the story of Merlin. After Vortigern has consulted his wise men he sends his knights searching the land to find a boy who has no father. They come one day to Carmarthen, and there they hear two children quarrelling. One is the king's son, and the other, as it happens, is Merlin.

They hear the king's son cry out in anger against Merlin:

'I am a king's son, and thou art born of nought;
Thou oughtest not in any spot, to have free men's abode.
For *so* was all the adventure, thy mother was a whore,
For she knew not ever the man that begot thee on her
Nor hadst thou any father among mankind.
And thou in our land makest us to be shamed
Thou art among us come and art son of no man.'

Obviously, Merlin is quite highly connected, otherwise he would not have been found playing with the king's son. And indeed they discover that he is the child of a princess; the daughter of King Conaan, who ruled over a third part of Wales. And she has taken the veil, and is a hooded nun, following the mysterious circumstances prior to Merlin's birth. Vortigern questions her about these circumstances, and in Layamon her account has a strange otherworldly beauty:

' "When I was fifteen years of age, in my mansion.
then dwelt I in bower, wondrously fair.
My maidens with me, with my soft sleep
And when I was in bed in slumber, the fairest thing that ever was born
then came before me arrayed all of gold.
as if it were a tall knight each night in sleep.
This I saw in dream and glistened of gold;
This thing glided before me and oft it me embraced;
oft it me kissed, and oft it came me very nigh;
oft it approached me, – strange this seemed to me –
When I at length looked to myself my limbs were strange
My flesh to me was loathsome what it might be!
Strange it seemed to me, that I was with child;
Then I perceived at the end this boy I had.
when my time came, what his father were
I know not in this world in this world's realm.
Nor who begat him or on God's behalf dight.
Nor whether it were evil thing I know not any more to say to thee
Alas as I pray for mercy of my son,

How he came into the world"
Then the nun bowed her head down and covered her features.'

60

This open mindedness on the mother's part is a stark contrast to the later French monkish accounts which assumed that Merlin's father must be a demon from hell, but that the devil had been foiled, by the pious mother entering a nunnery. They would have done better to take greater cognisance of the explanation of Magan, to whom King Vortigern sent.

'Magan was a marvellous man
He was a wise clerk,   and knew of many crafts
He would advise well,   he could far direct.
He knew of the craft that dwelleth
           in the sky,   he could tell of each the history.
Then said Magan: "I know full well hereon.
There dwell in the sky   many kind of beings
That there shall remain   until domesday arrive;
Some they are good,   and some they work evil.
Therein is a race very numerous,   that cometh among men
They are named full truly   Incubi Daemones.
They do not much harm   but deceive the folk
Many a man in dream   oft they delude
And many a fair woman   through their craft childeth anon.
And many a good man's child   they beguile through magic,
And thus was Merlin begot   and born of his mother
And thus is it all transacted"   quoth the clerk Magan.'

We need here to draw a distinction with the original Greek word *daimon* – meaning an extra terrestrial being – sometimes a communicator of wisdom, such as Socrates' daimon. The word and its meaning were later corrupted into 'demon', signifying an evil denizen of hell. The ecclesiastical mind had an unfortunate tendency to condemn and to denigrate that which it did not understand.

What *we* choose to call such beings is to a large extent arbitrary. As in human concerns, handsome is as handsome does. And in this context I cannot resist quoting the swingeing seventeenth century prose of the Abbé de Villars *Comte de Gabalis*, which treats much of these matters:

'People attribute to demons all that they should ascribe to the Elementary Peoples. A little Gnome was beloved by the celebrated Magdalen of the Cross, Abbess of a Monastery at Cordova in Spain. Their alliance began when she was twelve years of age; and they continued their relationship for the space of thirty years. An ignorant confessor persuaded Magdalen that her lover was a hobgoblin, and compelled her to ask absolution of Pope Paul III. It could not possibly have been a demon, however, for all Europe knew . . . the daily miracles wrought through the intercession of this holy maiden, and which obviously would never have come to pass if her relationship with the Gnome had been as diabolical as the venerable Dictator imagined.'

In Layamon, daemons are referred to as elves. As is well known from Malory, Merlin had much to do with the conception of Arthur and took charge of the child king. In Layamon, Merlin is closely connected with the elves.

I quote:

'There Uther the king took Ygaerne for queen;
Ygaerne was with child by Uther the king,
all through Merlin's craft before she was wedded.
The time came that was chosen then was Arthur born.
So soon as he came on earth, elves took him;
they enchanted the child with magic most strong,
they gave him might to be the best of all knights;
they gave him another thing, that he should be a rich king;
they gave him the third, that he should live long;
they gave to him the prince virtues most good,
so that he was most generous of all men alive.
This the elves gave him, and thus the child thrived.'

Merlin's antecedents, and those whom he worked with, were not of this world. This, and the elvish connections, places him in a similar condition to another manifestation of the archetype that has caught the imagination of the modern world. That is the wizard Gandalf in Tolkien's *Lord of the Rings*.

LINKS WITH GANDALF

In essence, and for the most part, Tolkien was working from the deep myth making imagination; and much in his stories, particularly in the Silmarillion, has a universal and fundamental validity. They are race memories, if you like, that he tapped into.

In all works of the practical use of the imagination, it is spiritual intention that is fundamentally important, and it was indeed Tolkien's avowed intention to create a body of English mythology. He says as much in a letter to the publisher Milton Waldman:

'I was from early days grieved by the poverty of my own beloved country; it had no stories of its own, (bound up with its tongue and soil), not of the quality I sought ... I had a mind to make a body of more or less connected legend ... which I could dedicate simply to England; to my country. It should possess the tone and quality that I desired, somewhat cool and clear, be redolent of our 'air' – the clime and soil of the north west, meaning Britain and the hither parts of Europe ...'

I think the evidence is that he succeeded and it is particularly worth our while to look to the figure of Gandalf as well as the figure of Merlin to delineate the essential features of the archetype on which they both are based.

Although Gandalf has the appearance of an old man, he is in fact of a higher or other world origination. He is one of the Istari, who came to Middle Earth in the Third Age to help human kind to counter the growing powers of evil.

Both Gandalf and Merlin, when they enter upon their destined work, work in much the same way. They do not solve the problems of humankind. But they set up conditions so that men and women can overcome their problems themselves.

Gandalf takes on the work involved in the formation of the Fellowship of the Ring, spurring and nudging various factions to work in concerted action – be they the half human hobbits, or the warriors of Gondor, or the Riders of Rohan. Merlin sets up the Fellowship of the Table Round, and takes care of the genetic engineering concerned with the birth of Arthur, setting him on the throne and providing him with his sword of destiny, Excalibur.

Their magic is of a higher kind than is found in their adversaries. In Merlin this is evident very early on when he is taken to the tower of Vortigern to be sacrificed. There he confounds all the wizards of the king by a clear demonstration of his superior knowledge and power. He diagnoses the cause of the problems of Vortigern's tower and goes from there into deep prophecies about the future of the land and of the nation – far in excess of Vortigern's immediate temporal preoccupations.

The king, who might well serve as archetype for modern corporate man, the chairman of World Exploiters International, deals summarily with his erstwhile magical senior management. He takes the senior one:

	and deprived him of his head,
and all his seven comrades	that were with him there.
And the king went to his house,	and had Merlin with him
and said to him with much love:	'Merlin thou art welcome,
and I will give thee all that thou	
desirest,	of my land, of silver, and of gold.'

He might today, have added – 'and a big cigar, and a company car, I'll make you a star.'

But as Layamon concludes: 'He weened through Merlin, to win *all* the land, but it happend all otherwise, ere the day's end came.'

Similarly, Gandalf's magic is of a different order to the magic of Sauron, the Dark Lord, and his minions. It is magic of a higher world, not of the corruption of the forces of a lower world. The distinction is made by the elven queen Galadriel to Frodo and Sam when she shows them her magic mirror during their stay in Lothlorien. She gently chides them for confusing high elf magic – which maintains her beautiful country – with the exploitative sorcery of the Enemy.

This corrupt and corrupting magic of the Dark Tower of Mordor is no better than the 'magic' that is practised today, not by the customers of the Atlantis Bookshop or Watkins, but by the image makers of the advertising industry, public relations, popular entertainment, sectarian propaganda, and all who manipulate, by what-

Figure 4   The Magician

ever means, the assumptions, perceptions, morals, and opinions of individuals and groups for corporate or political ends. Vortigern's magic, and Sauron's magic, and its modern equivalent, is based on exploitation and deception, and is nonetheless evil for being ostensibly well intentioned. Many a horror is perpetrated in the name of efficiency, cost effectiveness, rationalisation, law and order, or research. Not that these things are evil in themselves, but the criterion should be the end results for the weak and underprivileged. And these are easily subjugated to the demands of the machine, the corporation, the organisation, the system.

The higher magic provides no easy solutions to all of this, but it provides the only solution: the opening up of the lower worlds to the power, love and wisdom of the higher worlds. And the setting up of the channels to achieve this end is the function of the archetypal magician, of the Merlin, of the Gandalf. To the worldly wiseman he may appear somewhat eccentric, and even at times a failure or a fool. The magician bases his actions on the lineaments of a kingdom that is not of this world – and by the terms of his dedication he cannot impose or enforce his views. His tragedy, if tragedy it is, is that he has the means to save the world but only if the world will listen and take heed. In the meantime, he can only build bridges between the worlds and hope that some will cross them – in either direction. Then, having set up the pattern of the paths that he hopes will lead men to tread the right way, the magician has to withdraw from the scene of the action, something he may do in various ways, none of them easily understood by ordinary men, to whose limited or distorted perceptions it may only appear as a desertion, a weakness or a failure.

The image of the Tarot Trump of the Hanged Man strikes me as important in this regard. It depicts a man upside down – whose values are not of the everyday world. Thus, money, the life blood of the lower worlds, is sometimes seen falling from his hands or his pockets. Yet he seems content with his lot. And this card is also known as the Traitor. He has no allegiance to Mordor, to Mordred, or to Mammon.

Nonetheless, however much we think we realise and understand the necessity for the magician's withdrawal, it is with something of a shock that we read of Merlin's, or of Gandalf's, disappearance at a very early stage.

This happens surprisingly soon in the Arthurian stories as told by Sir Thomas Malory. The reader has a vague belief that Merlin is active all the way through, that his figure dominates a great deal of the action. However, in Caxton's edition, although the story runs to 21 books, Merlin disappears from the scene at the beginning of Book 4. From then on the young Arthur and his knights and ladies have to forge their destiny unaided, although helped indirectly by what Merlin has left in the form of hints and prophecies, and patterns of wisdom and action such as the Round Table, or various consecrated weapons and hallowed objects.

Gandalf likewise disappears into the depths of Khazad-dhum, in battle with a Balrog, when the companions of the Fellowship of the Ring are barely on their way. It then falls upon Aragorn, the hereditary king, and Frodo and Sam, the ring bearer and his companion, to see things through to a conclusion, to the best of their limited abilities. Only thus are forged the qualities of the dedicated, spiritually orientated human being, in the crucible of action in the world, on the basis of personal responsibility.

Gandalf is not inactive during his departure, in other spheres of influence, and he eventually returns in a higher form. And I doubt if Merlin is as dormant as the tale of Malory would have us think. He is not, I believe, a besotted swain in a flowery enchanted bower, but one who has entered the Earth, as many sacred kings and builders of bridges between the worlds are known to have done. I can only refer those sufficiently interested to Bob Stewart's *Underworld Initiation* for an outline of some of the dynamics of this profound and important subject.

THE HIDDEN STONE

The spiritual alchemists said: 'Visit the interior of the Earth — seek and rectify the hidden stone'. You will find this phrase in the frontispiece of the second volume of *The Western Way* by Caitlin and John Matthews; a practical guide to the Western Mystery Tradition that I sincerely believe will be one of the most important texts for students in the coming decade. I only wish I had written it myself, and that I had had such comprehensive and skilled advice when I was setting out.

This phrase is to be found encircling a diagram called The Emblem of the Great Work – which is also called the Philosopher's Stone. What is the stone of the philosophers, the stone of the lovers of wisdom? What are the hidden stones that we are enjoined to seek and rectify?

I would suggest that Gandalf, and Merlin, by their example, point the way to them. This is not a matter of intellectual speculation but of faith, spiritual intention, imagination, and experience. The Great Work in its wider implications is the Redemption of the Earth. And if I may quote Bob Stewart on this: 'Work of redemption is not dogmatically religious; it is a metaphysical and magical operation, not an evangelical crusade.'

But what of Mordor and the usurper kingdoms of Mordred or of Vortigern? What of the waste land that is all about us or of William Blake's Satanic mills?

Blake wrote of London:

I wander through each chartered street
Near where the chartered Thames does flow,
And mark in every face I meet
Marks of weakness, marks of woe.

In every cry of every Man,
In every infant's cry of fear,
In every voice, in every ban,
The mind forged manacles I hear.

How the Chimney-sweeper's cry
Every blackening church appalls;
And the hapless soldier's sigh
Runs in blood down palace walls.

But most thro' midnight streets I hear
How the youthful harlot's curse
Blasts the new born infant's tear,
And blights with plagues the marriage hearse.'

How would the 'chartered world' seek the hidden stone? By ripping out the bowels of the Earth, looking for the latest form of treasure – the fool's gold of uranium? Or sending the dark shadows of the fingers of its power heavenwards, in the colonisation of space? If so, the results may well be catastrophic.

I said above that magic is not just a cult pursuit of a few eccentrics who frequent certain London bookshops in Museum Street or Cecil Court – but is of the very fabric of life, though assuming different names. I would like to illustrate this by quoting from an editorial in *The Guardian* on Tuesday 11th June 1986. For it is really all about the magic of Mordor. It is talking about the Rogers report on the recent space shuttle disaster:

'There is only one way to read yesterday's devastating report on the destruction of the space shuttle Challenger: with bleak humility. Everything that could go wrong went wrong. Every system and every decent human instinct failed or floundered in bureaucracy. The seven astronauts did not go to their deaths; they were sent to their deaths, because safety routines were neglected for lack of cash, because the agency feebly bit off more than it could chew ...

'But nothing in Mr Rogers' 256 glossy pages lends credence to the belief that the *true* horror of Challenger – the human blend of *politics* and *patriotism* and *pressure* – can in any way be fundamentally addressed. Quite the contrary.

'Set the clinical passages of Rogers beside the eulogy that President Reagan delivered at mission control on the day after the disaster. "We promise Commander Dick Scobee and his crew that their dream lives on, that the future they worked so hard to build will become a reality ... (NASA) must forge ahead with a space programme that is effective, safe, efficient, but bold and committed."

'Not a word (how could there be?) for the men who, by their indifference, sloth and cowardice, made the dream tawdry. Not a thought for the *pressure* that such simplistic patriotism brings. It was a blend of that pressure, decked with PR trimmings, that sent Christa McAuliffe, the school teacher and mother of two children, to her death in Challenger; not as a heroine, but as a victim of the need to add a tabloid touch of glamour ...

'Toss Chernobyl into the account and there has been no grimmer period in modern history for high technology – with admitted "human error" linking East and West. Are there such things as space or nuclear power station programmes which are "safe and efficient" as well as "bold and committed"? ...

'NASA was in a triple bind: anxious to show results to keep the politicians sweet and the funds flowing; ham strung by plants strewn randomly across the pork barrel face of America; determined – in the profit-making business of satellite launches – to win contracts and present simultaneously the acceptable faces of heroism and capitalism. It all became too much. The agency simply cracked under the strain.

'And yet, within a year, the whips will be out again. America is more or less out of the satellite trade, whilst Mr Reagan unflaggingly pursues his own dream of Star Wars, an uninvented system of defence against nuclear attack which depends for its credibility on a level of technical efficiency that no country on earth – least of all his own country – has been able to attain.

'There *is* indeed a "dream" in space, a frontier which cannot be neglected or forgotten. But it is not, at heart, the dream of narrow politics, or national prestige; and if we continue to let it become so, then the sad pages of yesterday's report will be repeated time and again as we spread human vanities and human failings across the cosmos.'

The article begs the question: is it not an awareness of Merlin's inner earth that provides the real way for the world and the way *into* the Earth that really leads to the stars?

That may sound bizarre nonsense to those who wander blindly through the dark corridors of worldly power and material perceptions. But let us think of the young Merlin – and what *he* saw that Vortigern's magicians could not. The hidden stone, the secret lake, and the mighty contending dragon power, that lies beneath the dark tower. These are not psychological symbols, still less literary or historical allegories. They are images of a real and powerful world that exists beyond, and beneath, and indeed even supports our own. And which is capable of pulling down the constructions of the puny vanity of man, should it continue to be ignored. Merlin is an ambassador to and from that world. That is why the archetype of Merlin is so important for us today.

The Blue Stones of Merlin
by Gareth Knight

The more I examine the literary and mythological foundations of
the Arthurian legends, the more do I incline to the opinion that the
roots of British esoteric tradition lie in Wales. This was intuitively
supported by the general feel of things in a recent holiday to south-
west Wales – to what used to be called the county of Pembrokeshire
and which is now part of the anciently-named modern administrative
area of Dyfed.

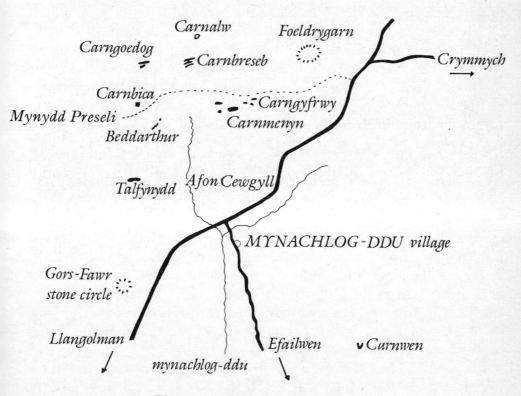

Figure 5   A Map of the Preseli Region

This part of our islands is particularly rich in geological interest, and geological considerations play a part in both the principal sacred centres that I visited. St David's Head, named after the patron saint of Wales, and site of one of our more evocative cathedrals, consists of some of the oldest rocks extant, dating from the pre-Cambrian period, some 4000 million years ago. And the inner circle of blue stones at Stonehenge have their source in the Preseli Mountains – though how they were transported is a matter of conjecture.

The general archaeological belief is that they were manhandled on rollers and transported on rafts over water. There is a river, the Afon Cewgyll, that runs below the ridge where the blue stones are to be found and it is conceivable that from thence they could have been floated into the river Taf and then by sea into the Bristol Channel and eventually to the river Kennet in Wiltshire. Some esoteric theorists think this idea implausible, however, and feel that some kind of Atlantean or pre-Celtic magic was used, perhaps connected with earth currents and geomagnetism. Needless to say, orthodox opinion considers this more unlikely than the cumbersome rollers and rafts method. Lately, a new geological theory rather takes the romance out of things by suggesting that the blue stones were carried quite naturally from Preseli to Salisbury Plain by a glacier, but by a return swing of the pendulum of scientific fashion, this idea has subsequently been doubted.

Merlin's connection is first recorded in the quasi-history of Geoffrey of Monmouth. As factual history, this ninth-century book is pretty comprehensively damned by professional historians, although it had enormous influence in its day and for several hundred years; and it is extremely important as a source and record of legendary material. There are of course different levels of truth; and legendary truth can be as important as the physical historical record. In fact, legend can encapsulate and give meaning to history. It is a record of the dynamics of the soul of a race. The pen is mightier than the sword, and the mythical imagination is mightier than the pen.

In Geoffrey's history, Merlin is said to have given orders to Uther Pendragon, Arthur's father, to fetch the stones and bring them to Stonehenge. In this record they are located in Ireland, but the confusion can be justified. This part of Wales might well have been under Irish domination or influence at the time – which must have been about 2000–1800 BC.

When one visits the area, one is immediately impressed that this is an important spot esoterically. In the plain before the mountains is a stone circle – said by the local guide books to be the only stone circle in Wales. This seems hard to credit, but if true suggests that a particular importance is attached to this site. The stone circle is not particularly impressive or massive as stone circles go, but it has a quality of peace and ancient calm about it such as I have experienced only in the rock temples of Hagar Qim and Menajdra in Malta, built contemporaneously with the circles of Stonehenge.

Around about one is a great semi-circle of mountains with jagged outcrops, so that one is reminded of the alternative title of Stonehenge: the Giants' Dance.

I am not naturally given to making meticulous measurements of ancient monuments and seeking alignments, but one alignment seemed particularly striking in that from one side of the stone circle of Gors-fawr, the stones line up with two large upright stones some hundred yards away that act as a kind of visual gateway to the outcrop of Carnmenyn whence the Stonehenge blue stones come.

About three-and-a-half miles north-east, the road crosses one of the most ancient trackways of Britain which wends its way across the tops of the Preseli Mountains. The views on a clear day must be tremendous; but upon the day I visited these were obscured by mist and low cloud.

Achieving the top of the blue stone outcrop could hardly have been more dramatic, however. Simultaneously there broke the most severe storm that had been experienced for years – the same that wrecked the Fastnet yacht race. Within seconds we were drenched to the skin in spite of waterproofs, a veritable baptism of total immersion!

On the way up, I had wondered why it was that the ancient track kept itself from being overgrown by the surrounding heather. Splashing our way down, I realised that it was because it acts as the bed of a gushing stream when the weather is wet. As if a thorough soaking were not enough, the mist then came down very heavily, reducing visibility considerably.

One then became aware of the possible use of a pair of aligned stones that we noticed on the way up. These pointed towards the high peak of Foeldrygarn, which is obscured from the stone circle of Gors-fawr by the ridge along which the ancient trackway goes, but which, when one is upon the trackway, towers imposingly as the King of the dancing giants.

The two standing stones just above the present Forestry Commission plantation are aligned to its peak. One realised, when the mist had come down and rendered visibility to less than twenty yards, that given the initial two-stone alignment, three men could find their way through dark and mist by aligning themselves with these stones – and then proceeding one by one, in turn, to the limits of visibility. By keeping in line with each other, they would arrive accurately at their destination.

These are but a few impressions of a visit that proved very esoterically interesting and worthwhile. The few fragments of blue stone we came down with have by no means denuded the extensive outcrops, and there is a fascinating structure and blue/green colouring to this intrusive igneous Ordovician dolerite rock – to give it its geological description. And probably by virtue of its being so far off the beaten track, the place is not swarming with the coach parties of visitors which mar the major sites of Southern England. In the old county of Pembroke – sometimes called 'the little England beyond Wales' – one sensed an esoteric meaning to the phrase, a sort of Logres in the West. It has the pure feel of the deepest roots of our island's spiritual destiny – like the Logres which C. S. Lewis and Charles Williams defended as being the secret, better, ideal part of prosaic England.

Merlin and Nimuë

by Gareth Knight

Following upon some intensive work on the Mysteries of the Goddess, the following came to me from a wise old hawthorn that I am accustomed to commune with on the elemental and nature contacts.

The tale in the Arthurian Legend of the enchantment of Merlin by Nimuë is, at root, a great cosmic myth of the star wizard and the earth maiden, in which can be comprised the history and destiny of the planet and the lives upon it.

In the legend, Merlin is the archetypal wizard or master of the wisdom whose function is to guide human evolution and establish patterns of civilisation. He thus appears at various moments to guide, warn or advise or take action at critical points – such as at the birth of Arthur or the endowment of the Round Table.

Part way though the story, he disappears, apparently enchanted by a fairy woman. He is never seen again, though there are reports of some who say they have heard his voice in the forest, imprisoned in an invisible tower.

There is no very satisfactory explanation for this strange event in the rather bald narrative of Malory, and nor does Tennyson's malignant Vivian ring true mythologically. More satisfactory clues are provided in the original prose *Merlin* translated from the French twenty-five years before Malory wrote *Le Morte d'Arthur*, and used by him as a source.

In the prose *Merlin*, Nimuë is a child of twelve years old. She is however in all her described qualities a young maiden, and the twelve may be regarded as a symbol of the zodiacal months of a whole year, and the maiden to be a form of Proserpine.

Her father is described as 'a vavasour of right high lineage, and his name was cleped Dionas, and many times Diana came to speak with him, that was the goddess, and was with him many days, for he was her godson'. This is a strong suggestion of the Dionysiac Mysteries as well as those of the goddess, and the two are indeed inter-related as appears at points in *The Golden Ass*.

Nimuë is brought up among the woods and rivers and Diana foretells that s' ʒ will win the love of the wisest man on earth.

The following account is taken from Chapter VI of *Le Morte d'Arthur of Sir Thomas Malory and its Sources* by Vida D. Scudder, a scholarly work, to our knowledge long out of print, but which certainly deserves republication for its lucid treatment of its subject, even though academically it may have been overtaken by more recent scholarship:

> 'So Merlin finds her, "in a valley under a mountainside round beside the forest of Briok, that was full delitable and fair, for to hunt at harts and hinds and buck and doe and wild swan". And he disguised himself as a fair young squire, "and drew him down to a well whereof the springs were fair and the water clear, and the gravel so fair that it seemed of fine silver". A pretty stage for the love-making. Nimuë comes often to this well to disport herself, and Merlin, half-ashamed, wistful, quite clear-sighted as to his folly, begins to lure the maiden gently by hinting at the great marvels he can show her. Eager and childish, she exclaims: "Certes these be quaint crafts and would that I could do such disports!" Whereupon he shows her such, and greater: for behold! Out of the forest comes a carole of ladies and knights and maidens and squires, "each holding other by the hands and dancing and singing: and made the greatest joy that ever was seen in any land"'.

Pleasant playthings for a little woodland maid! And presently, in the midst of the wild wood, appears an orchard, wherein was all manner of fruit and all manner of flowers, that gave so great sweetness of flavor that marvel it was to tell. So the delighted little lady tells Merlin, 'Fair sweet friend, you have done so much that I am all yours'. It is the most innocent of idylls, full of grace and charm. Lines in an old Welsh poem attributed to Merlin the bard hint at a similar tradition:

> 'Sweet apple-tree of delicate bloom
> That grows in concealment in the woods, ...
> While my reason had not strayed, I rested by its side
> With a fair gleeful maiden of perfect slender form'.

Classic grace and Celtic magic blend in the melodies that haunt these woods, and for the present the Holy Grail is quite forgotten. But before long little Nimuë begins to tease for full possession of her lover's knowledge. For the moment he satisfies her by giving her an obedient river for her slave, – 'the repaire of joy and feast,' and he leaves these plays and returns to his post, protector of the Round Table. But again and again he seeks his Nimuë, – who would not seek so sweet a thing? – and ever she entreats him never to leave her, till finally he yields. It is with full foreknowledge that Merlin tells the secret; when she spoke to him of her longing to know how to create the magic tower of air, he bowed down to the earth and began to sigh. None the less he did her will, and on a fateful day they went through the forest of Broceliande hand in hand, devising and disporting; and found a bush that was fair and high and of white hawthorn full of flowers, and there they sat in the shadow. And Merlin laid his head in the damsel's lap, and she began to caress gently till he fell on sleep, and when she felt that he was on sleep she arose softly, and made a circle with her wimple all about the bush, and all about Merlin. And when he waked he looked about him, 'and him seemed he was in the fairest tower of the world and the most strong; – and he said to the damsel: "Lady thou hast me deceived but if ye will abide with me, for none but ye may undo these enchantments"'. And in truth she stayed by him for the most part, 'Ye be my thought and desire', says she, 'for without you have I neither joy nor wealth. In you have I set all my hope, and I abide none other joy but of you'.

It is some comfort that her impulse is love, not as elsewhere malice or self-will. Perhaps Merlin was not so badly off after all. But the realm was in sad need of him, and never again did the fair order of chivalry thrive as it did while he watched over it.

'What indeed will become of the human children, deserted by Merlin in his fascination for Nimuë?' I asked the hawthorn.

'When Nimuë, the earth maiden has learned all the star lore of Merlin, and Merlin has learned the earth lore of Nimuë, then the two will go hand in hand in a cosmic marriage to the stars taking the children of earth with them.'

There was a strong image of the dark mantled Merlin in his robe and tall hat of stars, and the young floral and earthly maiden simply clad in the natural colours of earth.

There are parallels in the disciplines of classical ritual magic of the Qabalistic astro-celestial kind and the more homely lore of country Craft. The intellectualism of the one and the direct at-one-with-nature aspect of the other meet in complementary harmony.

One may also see parallels in myth and legend, from the early Egyptian myth of Isis discovering the secret name of Ra, and thenceforth being a mistress of enchantment, to the Genesis story of the Angels mating with the daughters of earth.

But to contemplate the images under a hawthorn may be a better way (rather than intellectual speculation), to gain wisdom of these matters.

PART 3
MERLIN IN MODERN FICTION

Introduction
by R.J. Stewart

The trivialising of Merlin in modern entertainment conceals a remarkable truth; he is as coherent in good fiction as in legend, despite the seeming paradox of his incoherency! When we see Merlin in cartoon form, as a comedy sketch in a TV panel game, or in more ambitious attempts at trivialisation such as the ill-fated Broadway musical, we see the work of people who have made no attempt to understand him, merely to use his name for superficial ends. Yet whenever an author has tried to reach an understanding of or with Merlin, as John Matthews shows in the following chapter, certain coherent elements always appear.

This does not imply that the coherence is in the mind of the author, nor that there is some 'master plan' instructing our imaginative works about Merlin, but there is no doubt that authors who make serious attempts at describing Merlin, even in science fiction form, tap into a set of images of enduring quality. Curiously, these images are not all drawn from the Merlin root material in early Celtic sources, nor from the Arthurian literature of the Middle Ages.

What are these images, and how do they relate to one another? A short summary would perhaps be as follows:

Merlin has three aspects. The bright youth; the mad prophet and shaman; the wise elder. All three are concerned with the interaction of spiritual and magical powers, with a strong emphasis upon a relationship with the land, the environment, and particularly the land of Britain.

Behind the aspects is a god-form. This deep and powerful image is, as John Matthews shows, given emphasis in the works of John Cowper-Powys and C. S. Lewis, though it also appears in many other approaches to Merlin, both published and private. This god-form, perhaps the primal deity discussed by Geoffrey Ashe in Chapter One guides or aids humanity through the triple expression described.

Thus Merlin, born of a mortal maiden and an otherworld spirit according to the chronicles, acts as the mediator for deep powers manifesting through the land into human consciousness. His three-fold appearance is initially that of the lifetime of any person; youth, adulthood, maturity, but into each of these aspects is channelled the most potent dynamic power, imagery, and mystery of each life phase.

As a youth, he is the eternal child, of spiritual purity; as a mature man he is the wild fervent power of magic or transforming consciousness; as an elder he is the epitome of wisdom, learning, transcendant knowledge, and of course experience. In fictional works unconnected to one another, this coherence out of diversity is apparent; and occasionally the deep ancient god-form appears, the non-human power behind the semi-human Merlin. This power may also take a number of shapes, but what is remarkable is that authors of quite different style, cultural background and quality of work may be imaginatively aware of its existence.

There is no chronicle source for Merlin as a god or titanic power, only a few hints in early Welsh poetry. Later romances and chronicles were divided between the magician of Arthur's court and the increasingly orthodox image of a diabolical being – though there is no mention of Merlin linked to Arthur in the early sources, and certainly no question of evil. As has been discussed repeatedly during our other chapters, a *daemon* is not the same as a *demon*. The first is a guiding and instructing spirit (such as inspired Socrates) well known in classical allusions and cosmology, while the second is the product of Judaeo-Christian propaganda and subtle editing. Yet this confusion has brought modern writers into contact with the image that is at the foundation of the figure of Merlin ... a mysterious primal god or tutelary being.

In primal cultures, the wise man or *shaman* (to use an increasingly popular term which should perhaps be limited to its Siberian cultural origins) acts as the vehicle for spiritual power, which may manifest itself in derivative forms, such as spirits or totem animals, or may occur in its own right, albeit filtered through human consciousness. Both of these elements of mediation or priesthood, known in all cultures and religions worldwide, are present in the Merlin legends.

In the *Vita Merlini* of Geoffrey of Monmouth, shamanistic Celtic and spiritual religious elements are intentionally fused together, with Merlin growing through his wild prophetic fervour towards a spiritual retirement in an astrological observatory in the woods. Geoffrey was clearly aware that the aspects or faces of Merlin need not be contradictory, but are highly energised presentations of changes and modes of consciousness shared by all men and women.

The other significant element dealt with at length by Geoffrey, is that of sexuality or polarity. The entire *Vita* is an adventure reaching from the personality to the universe, and guided at all stages by sexual or polarised relationships. These are catalysed by the figure of Ganieda (Merlin's sister) who is very similar to Minerva or the Celtic Briggidda; a number of other women also appear in the role of pleasant or vengeful lovers, and of course as the famous priestess and shape-changer Morgen who cares for the wounded King Arthur in the Fortunate Isle.

Sexuality is naturally a central subject for writers of fiction; although after the perverted post-medieval role ascribed to Woman in Mallory, and to a much greater extent in Tennyson, it is sometimes difficult to grasp the essence of Merlin's relationship to women.

As all of the examples cited by John Matthews deal in varying ways with the theme of sexuality or polarity, we should examine briefly how this theme connects to the primal myths of universal creation, for this is where the key to Merlin and Woman may be found. (The following is merely a summary of a subject which demands a separate study in its own right.)

Merlin's love of women, sometimes moralised into a sexual weakness, is a reflection of his otherworldly father's love for his mother. This in turn relates to one of the most ancient mythical themes, and like all Merlinic lore is intimately concerned with both environment and the spiritual intimations found in all religions, magic, and mysticism. Traditionally, spirits of a certain order 'between the moon and the Earth' are said to advise men and women, hear their prayers and convey them to divinity, and to join in love with mortal women.

This theme is merely a microcosmic or lesser reflection of a great religious motif; it finds its epitome in the Virgin Birth, known in many religions but refined and featured in Christianity. In short, divinity joins with humanity. In pagan religions, this was part of the procreation and fertility of the earth, while in Christianity it has become tidied up by successive schools of scholarship and moralising Church Fathers who wished to cut their congregation off from other cults.

Gnostic worshippers, fusing pagan and early Christian wisdom, knew full well that the appearance of Christ within the world was a sexual matter, and the mystical adoration of the Saviour in later writings, prayers and meditative practices leaves us in no doubt as to the potentially sexual quality of otherworldly inspiration. This does not imply, and never has implied, a physical or gross element to such spiritual realisations; merely that if they are to be true, they must be true on all levels.

In the Old Testament and many other mythical books or tales, we have the famous legend of angels who copulated with mortal women, breeding a race of giants upon earth. Once again, this, like later variants of the Merlin legend, has become corrupted into a wilful misrepresentation of sexuality; it is really a myth reflecting certain stages of the relationship between humanity and divinity. In orthodox Christian religion, it is God's love of the World that causes Christ to be sent as a Saviour.

The fall of Lucifer into the earth, the love of angels for mortal women, the impregnation of a virgin, the relationship between humankind and the land, and the love of God for Humankind, are all woven together inextricably . . . for they are part of the polarity pattern of existence. We could define this pattern in mythical and religious terms, as above, or in psychological jargon, or in the formulae of science, but whatever words we choose to use the truth is undeniable; the mysteries of life are mysteries of polarity. For us, polarity is usually sexual in the most individual or personalised sense, but for otherworldly beings (be they daemons on one level or Divinity upon another) the personal reflection is absent, and sexuality partakes of a transcendant metaphysical quality, while including physical manifestation.

Thus the various sexual convolutions of Merlin in modern fiction are not merely misunderstandings or corruptions of the source material (in which the sexual weakness, sin, evil or grossly sensual

Figure 6   The Three Faces of Merlin

elements are not to be found) but are explorations of a universal theme expressed through the mediating figure of Merlin.

Finally, John Matthews' chapter suggests, subtly, something rather remarkable about fiction that deals with Merlin. We opened this introduction with criticism of the trend towards trivialising myth in modern entertainment, a trend that is by no means confined to the figure of Merlin. John Matthews shows, however, that even quite outrageous and perhaps poorly written treatments of Merlin in almost any context can carry within them the primal mythic elements that contribute to the protean figure of the prophet, magician, and wise man. What, we may ask, is the difference? Why do some treatments of Merlin fail utterly and even inspire revulsion, while others, poor as they may be, speak truth?

Merlin in Modern Fiction
by John Matthews

'Because I am dark and always shall be, let my book be dark and mysterious
in those places where I will not show myself.'

This passage, from a medieval text about Merlin, makes a good
point from which to begin this brief exploration, because it exactly
describes what has happened. In no two versions is Merlin ever the
same – even allowing for the idiosyncrasies of the various authors
who have written about him, the divergence is so great that it would
be difficult to imagine that it was the same character were it not for
certain basic common factors which, ultimately, seem to reveal the
figure at the heart of this constellation of disguises.

Merlin has remained 'dark and mysterious' despite everything.
Yet somehow, none of those who have chosen to write about him
have been able to resist asking the question: who – or what – is
he? Their answers have been as diverse as they possibly could be,
picturing Merlin as god or jester, as prophet, wiseman and sage; as
an old lover caught in the silken wiles of his young pupil; as an alien
being, brought to earth on cosmic business; as a wondrous child or
an Atlantean priest; as a servant of many gods or of one Goddess;
as a charlatan and a liar and a madman. But always, between the
disguises, we glimpse another face, that of a grey-clad pilgrim and
wanderer, sent here long ago to guide and guard the destiny of kings
and of men – a majestic mage steering the barque of the island that
has been named after him: Clas Merdin – Merlin's Enclosure, or

'Merlin's isle of Gramarie
Where you and I will fare.'
                    Kipling

and with whose destiny his own is inextricably linked.

We perhaps know Merlin best in his most familiar guise – as the wise and foresighted wizard who stands behind Arthur in the early days of his reign and who acts as advisor and councillor to the young king until he himself is ensnared by a beautiful young woman who becomes his apprentice. Modern fictional versions of this basic tale do exist, but it is at some less familiar aspects that I wish to look here, in the belief that an examination of the many facets of Merlin's character which they portray, will throw some light on the *real* Merlin, the enchanter in hiding.

ATLANTEAN ORIGINS

The span of his years is certainly immense; possibly, like Melchizedek, 'without beginning or end.' Surprisingly, few writers of this or any age have looked for his beginnings. It is in the writings of the esotericist Dion Fortune (1890–1946) that we first find mention of Merlin as an Atlantean priest who fled from the destruction of the lost continent, bearing with him the princess Igraine, destined to become the mother of Arthur. Though Dion Fortune wrote no novel of Merlin himself, this idea has surfaced in two recent books of very different quality: *The Mists of Avalon* (1982) by Marion Zimmer Bradley, and *Merlin and the Dragons of Atlantis* (1983) by Rita and Tim Hildebrandt. In the latter, Merlin is a scientist from Lemuria, a land adjacent to Atlantis and far older. It has adopted more peaceful and mystical ways than those of its more powerful neighbours, who now seek to perfect a race of genetically-engineered dragons to protect their vast cities and great domains. Merlin's thirst for knowledge brings him to join those working on the project, but when it is successful and the dragons are subsequently taken over by evil forces, he helps to destroy them, bringing about also the premature fall of Atlantis and the destruction of all that he loves. But Merlin himself does not die; he places himself in an induced state of hibernation from which he will wake to bring about the realization of a new dream, the creation of a new Atlantean state within the world of the Arthurian heroes. Then, we are told:

'he found his child and taught him well. The child grew with wisdom and knowledge into manhood. Thus for a brief second in history Merlin saw Arthur have his Camelot'

(p. 105)

Dragons of Atlantis represents an effort to show Merlin as a transcendent figure, able to operate over vast distances of time, through the use of knowledge no longer current in our world. Atlantis is merely the latest image of the Otherworldly realm from which Merlin has always been recognised as coming, while the image of Merlin himself is much as we would expect him to be portrayed in our time: as a scientist rather than as a wizard or seer; as someone imbued with endless curiosity about the nature of creation and its foremost offspring: mankind.

Marion Bradley's book is both well-written and imaginatively satisfying, though, for her, Merlin is a title borne by many rather than a name belonging to any one figure. Here, as in numerous recent versions of the story, the setting is post-Roman Britain, in which Merlin acts as an agent of those who seek to unite the shattered country into an unshakable force under the banner of Arthur. But already, before that dream is even begun, a deeper split exists – a religious division between Christianity and those who follow the way of the Goddess of Earth. Bradley's interpretation seems to say more about the current spiritual divide between orthodox religion and eco-pagan groups than about any actual spiritual divisions existing in post-Roman culture. Nevertheless, her personal colouring of events gives the book it vigour and also allows her Merlin to voice a genuine observation:

'There are now two Britains ... their world under their One God and the Christ; and beside it and behind it, the world where the Great Mother still rules, the world where the Old People have chosen to live and worship.'

(p. 15)

Igraine, soon to be the mother of the young king, remembers an earlier time, an earlier incarnation. In a waking vision, she stands on Salisbury Plain and watches the fiery sun rise over the great stone circle – and beyond,

'To the West, where stood the lost lands of Lyonesse and Ys and the great isle of Atlas-Alamesios, or Atlantis, the forgotten kingdom of the sea. There, indeed, had been the great fire, there the mountain had blown apart, and in a single night, a hundred thousand men and women and little children had perished.

"But the Priests knew" said a voice at her side. "For the past hundred years, they have been building their star temple here on the plains, so that they might not lose count of the tracking of the seasons ... These people here, they know nothing of such things, but they know we are wise, priests and priestesses from over the sea, and they will build for us, as they did before"...'

(p. 63)

The speaker is Uther, who shares Igraine's reincarnational memories. From their love is soon to issue the young Arthur who with Merlin's aid will try to build a new and perfect expression of Human endeavour. Here, we may see Merlin as representing the latest of a line of priests descended from the long-ago escapees of the doomed land, who have carried the seeded memories of the past within them until it can be brought once again into manifestation.

In a different way this is the aim of Merlin in Andre Norton's *Merlin's Mirror* (1975), where the image is a creation of a race of alien beings known as the Sky Lords, who in the infancy of the world leave behind them a hidden computer installation programmed to begin its work many thousands of years later, by the creation of heroes and leaders who will raise the race of men to their own height. There is an implication also that the Sky Lords will themselves have perished by this time, perhaps as a result of a long struggle with an opposing force called 'the Dark Ones'. These are not intrinsically evil, it seems, but are opposed to the actions of the Sky Lords and their aim to hasten the development of humanity.

In this science fiction version of the story, Merlin is created by means of the artificial insemination of a British woman who sees only a computer-generated image of a beautiful golden man – an ingenious twist to the story of Merlin's birth in Geoffrey of Monmouth's twelfth century *Historia*. But, just as Merlin represents the Sky Lords, so are the Dark Ones represented by Nimue, and the ancient destiny of the King, his wizard, and the priestess who brings about their downfall, is here played out in images drawn from the cosmic world of the science fiction novel. In the end, Merlin, who has read all the future in his computer-operated 'mirror', sees that his dream of a united land under the figure of Arthur, is doomed to fail, and he retires, like the Merlin of the Hildebrand novel, into a self-induced sleep to await a more auspicious time when he may try again.

In Susan Cooper's *Dark is Rising* sequence (1965–1979) we are afforded a glimpse of Merlin once again in immortal guise, as a combatant against the powers of evil. To the world at large he is known as Dr Merriman Lyon, a professor of Arthurian studies and an archaeologist – two roles we may well imagine Merlin adopting in a twentieth-century setting. In reality, however, he is one of an immortal race known simply as 'the Old Ones', whose endless task it is to combat the ancient forces of the Dark. This is more openly dualistic than either Andre Norton or C. S. Lewis, but as in both of these writers, and in the work of the Hildebrandts there are echoes of Merlin's Atlantean origins. Once again his task is to guide the steps of human protagonists – here a group of children – rather than directly intervene in the age-old war of Light and Dark. As in his guidance of the young Arthur in the original romances, this role is one which requires him to adopt many faces and forms, becoming elusive and secret and unfathomable in order to perform his task.

MERLIN'S PRIMARY TASK

We have seen already that Merlin is often shown to be a priest or councillor of kings, who comes from a far-off land where civilisation, or knowledge, may be more advanced than in the rest of the world. We can be sure as well that he is possessed of occult or prophetic knowledge, and we can extend our understanding of his role or function further by turning to another Merlin-type figure, who does not bear his name but who occupies a position in almost every way the same as that taken by Merlin. The relevant passage goes thus:

'Warm and eager was his spirit ... opposing the fire that devours and wastes with the fire that kindles and succours in wan hope and distress; but his joy, and his swift wrath, were veiled in garments grey as ash, so that only those who knew him well glimpsed the flame that was within. Merry he could be and kindly to the young and simple, and yet quick at times to sharp speech and the rebuking of folly; but he was not proud, and sought neither power nor praise, and thus far and wide he was beloved among all those that were not themselves proud. Mostly he journied unwearyingly on foot, leaning on a staff; and so he was called among men of the North Gandalf, the "Elf of the Wand".'

J. R. R. Tolkien: *Unfinished Tales* pp. 390–1

Gandalf, of course, in Tolkien's mythology, is one of the Istari, emissaries of the Valar, great angelic forces who watch over the world and mediate between God and creation. This is completely in line with the primary task allotted to Merlin in the majority of the stories about him – to guide and shepherd the destinies of men. It is in this guise that we encounter him again and again, both in the medieval stories, and in the writings of modern authors – books as varied and far apart in scope as John Cowper Powys' *Porius*, (1951), Mary Stewart's Merlin trilogy (1970–1979), Peter Vansittart's *Lancelot* (1978), and Linda Halderman's fantasy *The Lastborn of Elvinwood* (1980).

The Merlin of Porius, is half-man and half-god, a huge, slow earth-man, smelling of mould and green things. His work is devoted to the return upon earth of a new Golden Age, the age of Saturn/Cronos, of which god he sees himself as a true avatar. Descriptions of him abound in Powys' extraordinary book. Here is just one:

'Myrddin Wyllt was dressed in his long black mantle; and at the place where his great beard reached the level of his navel, it was tied with the usual gold thread whose tassels hung down to his knees. His head was bare, and his long fingers at the end of his long arms were making slow majestic movements as if writing upon the interior darkness of the tent ... But it soon occurred to Porius that what the man was doing lent itself to another and quite different interpretation; namely, that instead of inscribing things on the air he was *tracing out things* that had already been written upon it!'

(p. 405)

Powys' Myrddin Wyllt (or the Wild) is linked specifically with an ancient race of aboriginal giants, the very children of Cronos it seems, of whom the last remnant live out their days in the fastness of Welsh mountains. In Linda Halderman's book, Merlin is again associated with the destiny of a race of huge people – though here they have remained hidden, and have dwindled, becoming in time a smaller race, the denizens of Faery, who have no love for he whom they call 'the Old One', blaming his actions in a dim and distant time for their own present state. Their traditions tell how once their giant ancestors

'... dwelt in the mountains to the north mostly, herding and farming and minding their own business. He, the Old One, lived alone in the south. What he is and where he came from, I cannot say. Perhaps your legend of him being the offspring of a demon has some truth in it. I don't pretend to know. We call ourselves the First Folk, because it is our belief that our gigantic ancestors were the first people to live on this island. Yet they called him the Old One [even then].'

(p. 136)

The present day heroes, seeking to enlist his aid in the matter of two changelings, find the Old One living in semi-retirement in a cottage in the depths of the English countryside. On their way to visit him they discuss his history – the story of his being the son of the devil, and of his entrapment by Nimue:

'Ah yes, Nimue ... A naive ruse, but one that worked. It was the end of what he calls his political phase ... Arthur turned out to be a bitter disappointment, more interested in holding bloody tournaments than in planting gardens, [Merlin's great love] ... and unnaturally preoccupied with his wife's activities ... Arthur is one of the main reasons he's down on the Celts ... he decided to retire. Arthur refused to let him go, so he paid Nimue to invent the cave story and slipped off to live in blissful solitude ...'

(p. 64)

Here we have a glimpse of a lighter side of Merlin's nature, yet he is still a difficult and even a dangerous character, who can be both chancy and unreliable in his dealings with humanity. Peter

93

Vansittart, in his novel of Lancelot, paints an even more oblique portrait. Here, Merlin is generally referred to as 'He' – a mark of respect and caution towards the Old One, whom one should never address by name unless invited to do so. 'He' seems, at first glance, an unprepossessing character:

'Despite the familiar dirt caking his ears, beard, bare feet, the sacklike gown under gaudy robes, he repelled me less, his hierophantic mendacities more lively than the dismal hush that passed for entertainment with Artorius. Last year his hand motions had induced a snowfall when least required, his explanations being acceptable as minor poetry by anyone without scholarship or sensitivity. He had also acquired an adroit method of inclining his head so that a shadow of a bird or animal was reflected on the wall behind him.'

(p. 144)

THE PROPHET

Merlin's prophetic gifts are so much a part of his character that they almost seem to pass unnoticed at times, though it is by this means that he is enabled, primarily, to bring about the shaping of the destiny of others. Mary Stewart, in her trilogy of books about Merlin (*The Crystal Cave, The Hollow Hills* and *The Last Enchantment*) makes these powers central.

In the first volume, Merlin discovers his ability to 'see' future events; but his visions are the product of fits brought on by staring into a pattern of crystals, rather than by inner or magical contact, and throughout the remainder of the book and those which follow it, ingenious solutions are found for many of the more mysterious aspects of Merlin's life. Thus we read nothing of his magic, only of his technical skills, which enable him to position the 'Hele Stone' of Stonehenge at its present site, rather than (as in the medieval stories) raising the whole monument or causing it to fly through the air or float across the Irish Sea.

This portrait of Merlin succeeds in flattening out the character in an effort to explain it – psychological motivation accounting for most of his life – though he remains a prime mover in the setting up of a stable kingdom under the enlightened rule of Arthur.

The third volume of the trilogy recounts the relationship with Nimue – almost the only attempt to tell this story fully since Tennyson debased it to Victorian drawingroom melodrama in his *Merlin and Vivian* of 1890. In Mary Stewart's version, with Arthur established as king over all of Britain, Merlin retires to the wilderness. There, attacked by a subtle poison administered to him by Morgause, he is nursed back to health by a youth named Ninian, who of course turns out to be a girl, Niniane, or Nimue:

> 'The dim-seen figure in the mist, [seemed] so like the lost boy, that I had greeted her and put the words 'boy' and 'Ninian' into her head before she could even speak. Told her I was Merlin: offered her the gift of my power and magic, gifts that another girl – the witch Morgause – had tried in vain to prise from me, but which I had hastened eagerly to lay at this stranger's feet.'

> (p. 365)

THE LOVER

Thereafter, the story follows the more familiar track. Nimue becomes Merlin's pupil – until in the end, his powers begin to fade and she takes over the role of guardian of Arthur's realm. Finally, Merlin himself withdraws, promising to return. His end is left uncertain.

The only other significant treatment of Merlin as a lover, is in a book by the American author, James Branch Cabell. Cabell is something of an oddity amongst those who have dealt with Arthurian themes in fiction in that he sets his book, *Something About Eve* (1935), within the framework of a huge invented universe of chivalry and the erotic, spanning vast areas of time and space. In a chapter entitled 'The Chivalry of Merlin', the old wizard is summoned, along with King Solomon and Odysseus, to give an account of himself before he passes 'into the realms of Antan' (Cabell's name for the Otherworld), to discover the true meaning of his life:

95

'I was Merlin Ambrosius. The wisdom that I had was more than human ... but I served heaven with it ...' And then Merlin told about the child Nimue who was the daughter of the goddess Daina, and of how old, wearied, overlearned Merlin had come ... [to love her]. Then Merlin told to Nimue, because she pouted so adoringly, the secret of building a tower which is not made of stone, or timber, or iron, and is so strong that it may never be felled while this world endures. And Nimue, the moment he had fallen asleep with his head in her lap, spoke very softly the old rune ...'

(p. 190)

And Merlin confesses that he was happy for a long while in his tower, until he saw his 'toys', the men and women of the Arthurian age, begin to break each other and to become filled with hate and lust and barbarity. But even then he lingers on, happy with his child love and the peace of his tower – only now does he seek enlightenment in the Otherworld, where perhaps he may find reasons for the failure of his dream ...

For, whatever Merlin's end, whatever his origins, he never ceases to be concerned with this world and the people who live in it. His function within what we may call the 'inner history' of Britain varies hardly at all from Geoffrey of Monmouth to Mary Stewart. As the prime mover in the setting up of Arthur's kingdom, and of the Round Table; and as prophet, guardian and sometime tutelary spirit of Britain, he remains true.

Thus, in Parke Godwin's *Firelord* (1980), when he assumes another guise, that of the Wonder-Child, it is to offer Arthur some cursory advice:

'The boy was seated on a flat rock ... He looked maddingly familiar with his shock of blond, curly hair and blue eyes glistening with secret excitement: things to do and tomorrows that couldn't be caught up fast enough. He *shimmered* all over, he made me tingle with the energy that came from him ...'

(pp. 5–6)

Here, Merlin is, in some sense, Arthur's own inner self, able to show him a vision of the future, of the great king and warrior whose presence draws the very utmost effort from the men who follow him – the man that Arthur is to become, driven by the Merlin within:

'Deep in me, Artos stirs.

Stay away, I tell him. Go back to sleep.

But Artos wakes . . . opens his eyes inside me. "It's time" he says.

Time for what?

"I know what Merlin wanted to teach me," whispers Artos in my soul.

"To be a king over men. To know what they are and the price of knowledge."'

(p. 84)

THE TEACHER

Merlin's function is indeed often to teach – though he may choose to do so in some curious ways. In T. H. White's *The Sword in the Stone* (1938), he teaches by example, turning Arthur into animal, fish or bird. So that, from his encounter with a great pike that lives beneath the walls of his foster-father's castle, he learns that power for its own sake leads nowhere; while from a position high above the earth, Arthur as a bird discovers that boundaries are an illusion fought over without reason. And of course, all that he learns stands him in good stead when he comes to draw the famous sword from the stone – the act that will make him King:

'All round the churchyard there were hundreds of old friends. They rose over the church wall all together, like Punch and Judy ghosts of remembered days, and there were otters and nightingales and vulgar crows and hares and serpents and falcons and fishes and goats and dogs and dainty unicorns and newts and solitary wasps and goat-moth caterpillars and cockindrills and volcanoes and mighty trees and patient stones. They loomed round the church walls, the lovers and helpers of the Wart (Arthur) and they all spoke solemnly in turn . . .'

(pp. 279–80)

Nor is it surprising that Merlin should choose this method of teaching. His earliest incarnation was as the Wild Herdsman, the Lord of the Beasts, and even the trees and stones obey his call.

But it is as tutor and guide to the young king that we know him best, and as such he appears again and again in modern retellings. Catherine Christian in her excellent *The Sword and the Flame* (1982) has him arranging for Arthur to acquire his second, more famous sword, Excalibur. But in a variation from the more traditional episode, where he receives it from the Lady of the Lake, here Merlin assists in its forging by an ancient Smith God, from a lump of meteorite:

> 'It is now (says Merlin). Listen, Old One, the stream sings for it. The fire-spirits call for it. Fetch the King-sword here, to the anvil, and finish its forging, while the power of the Dragon and the power of the Merlin are together in this place to give you strength.'

(p. 52)

That the shaping of King or sword may extend beyond a single lifetime is shown in those versions of the story where Merlin or Arthur come again, after a long sleep, in Avalon or the Hawthorn Tower, to continue the work left unfinished at the end of the Arthurian Age. In the final part of C. S. Lewis' science fiction trilogy (*That Hideous Strength* [1945]), Merlin is awakened by the striving of the forces of good and evil – here represented by Ransom, Lewis' space voyager, and a totalitarian group seeking control over the earth. Here, somewhat as in Powys' version, Merlin is seen as almost a god – a force as old as time itself; a massive, primitive power virtually without limit. When he and Ransom first meet there follows a marvellous riddling exchange in which each tests the knowledge of the other. When Ransom has successfully answered a whole string of questions, Merlin asks another which he deems even harder: where is Arthur's ring?

> '"The Ring of the King," said Ransom, "is on Arthur's finger where he sits in the House of Kings in the cup-shaped land of Abhalljin, beyond the seas of Lur in Peralandra. [Lewis' name for Venus.] For Arthur did not die; but Our Lord took him to be in the body until the end of time ... with Enoch and Elias and Moses and Melchisedec the King. Melchisedec is he in whose hall the steep-stoned ring sparkles on the finger of the Pendragon."'

(p. 337)

Ransom is thereafter revealed as Arthur's successor, the new Pendragon, to whom Merlin once again pledges his service, and whom he aids in the final overthrow of the modern day forces of evil.

Figure 7   Merlin, the Oldest Man

References to Numinor (sic) and the 'Far West' in this book confirm the identification of Merlin with Gandalf in Tolkien's *Lord of the Rings*.

REINCARNATION

The theme of the recurring acts of Merlin and Arthur is taken up again by the science fiction writer Tim Powers in *The Drawing of the Dark* (1977). Here, Merlin is the guardian of the Wounded Grail King, who is kept alive, by a curious twist of the old story, not though the daily descent of a dove bearing a wafer in its beak, but by a yearly draught of a unique elixir – Hertzwestern Beer! Merlin, the owner of the inn where this mysterious drink is brewed, recalls the latest incarnation of Arthur in the shape of a seventeenth-century Irish mercenary named Brian Duffy, to help him protect the elixir against an ancient and implacable enemy. The substance of the book is concerned with Duffy's adventures and with his unwillingness to allow memories of himself as Arthur to come to the surface. But throughout the story the figure of the old magus moves subtly. He is old, here, an undying figure who seems eternally destined to pit himself against the enemies of light.

In this guise also, he reappears in a children's book, *Merlin's Magic*, by Helen Clare (1953). Here Merlin calls upon figures as diverse as Walter Raleigh, Morgan-le-Fay, Francis Drake and the Greek god Mercury to aid him in frustrating an invasion of Robot-people who, because they lack the essential human function of the imagination, seek to steal it from mankind. Were they successful, Merlin implies, he himself, as well as Arthur and the other great figures, once mortal but now transformed into mythic archetypes, would all fade. The resulting loss to humanity would, of course, be almost without equal, and it is up to the great wizard to save the day again!

THE TRICKSTER

Despite Powys' version, which comes near to it, we lack a truly shamanistic novel of Merlin. However, Merlin the trickster is not unrepresented. Apart from Linda Halderman's book there are two others: Robert Nye's *Merlin* (1978), and to a lesser extent, Thomas Berger's *Arthur Rex* (1979), which both deal with this strange, untoward side of the magus' nature.

Berger is closest in many respects to Malory's version, though his book is a comic masterpiece shot through with gleams of the high fantasy of the original Arthuriad. In a scene near the beginning of the book, two knights seek out Merlin at an enchanted fountain in the forest:

'And both the knight and the horses, being sore thirsty, drank from the crystal water of the spring (into which one could see forever because there was no bottom) and by the time they had soaked their parched throats the men had been transformed into green frogs and the horses into spotted hounds.

Now in despair and confusion the knights clambered with webbed feet from the steel armour which had fallen around them as they diminished in size, and the horses howled in dismay.

"None may drink of my water without my leave," said a voice, and looking aloft the frogs saw it was the raven that spake.

Then the glossy black bird flapped his wings twice and before their bulging eyes he was transformed into a man with a long white beard and wearing the raiment of a wizard, which is to say a long gown, a tall hat in the shape of a cone, both dark as the sky at midnight with here and there twinkling stars and a hornèd moon. And the next instant Merlin (for it was he) caused both knights and horses to return to their proper forms and only then did he laugh most merrily.'

(p. 3)

Nye, on the other hand, aiming for a comedy of Eros, plumbs the depths of Merlin's character, as very few writers have managed to do. I make no secret of the fact that this is almost my favourite portrait of Merlin. It is funny, irreverent and profound, and underneath its scatalogical humour and endless word-play, there is a deeply-researched picture which draws upon nearly all the many disguises of Merlin to reveal him, at last, as a strangely sorrowful creature, mourning for the even more sorrowful creatures over whom he has been given care.

From within the crystal cave of his retirement, Merlin views past, present and future with a jaundiced eye. He describes himself as:

> 'Merlin Ambrosius. Merlin Sylvester.
> Merlin the magician. Merlin the witch.
> The wisest man at the court of King Arthur,
> and the greatest fool. Well, shall we say the only *adult*.
>
> . . .
>
> My mother was a virgin.
> My father was the devil.'

(p. 3)

For Nye, this is the crux of the matter – Merlin partakes of *both* natures – human and non-human, good and evil, god and devil. Within him are the legions of hell and the armies of heaven. He is the battleground and the object of conquest and defence: ourselves – humanity. It is part of the subtle alchemy of Nye's book that he is able to show up the black side of human nature – as well as its silly side: all libido and bluster – and yet give a sense of the triumph of man over his own shortcomings. Merlin is the *deus ex machina* who stands ready to intervene, who laughs and plays the fool but who, underneath, *cares* for his children.

It is virtually impossible to get a proper feeling of Nye's book from a quotation – you have to read it all. Here are just two short extracts from the beginning and end of *Arthur*:

> 'The boyhood of Arthur. The madness of Merlin.
>   Look.
>   A golden-haired boy running through a deep golden pool of sunlight falling into the trees in the deepest deep of the wild green wood.
>   Arthur running through the golden and the green.
>   His golden hair. His green tunic.
>   "Sometimes you seem mad, or a fool, or a boy like me."
>
> . . .
>
> I teach him. Merlin teaches Arthur.
>   To KNOW

To DARE
To WILL
To KEEP SILENT.
Arthur is not a good pupil ...'

(p. 150–152)

And at the end:

'They bare away Arthur no man knows where.
(Unwise the thought: a grave for Arthur.)
The first queen has the face of the Virgin Vivien.
The second queen has the face of the Lady Igrayne.
The third queen has the face of the King's half-sister, Queen Morgan le Fay.
   Now without a sail, without oars, the draped barge passes out from the shore.
It is black upon the waters, and then gold.
Little pig, listen.
The wind in the reeds.
The laughter of Merlin!'

(p. 211)

There are echoes here of Malory, Geoffrey of Monmouth, old Welsh poetry and tradition, and even Tennyson.

A DEFINITIVE PORTRAIT

No one book has yet appeared which attempts to deal with all the aspects of Merlin's character, and perhaps there could be no such book. Robert Nye comes closest in my opinion, and there is the recent collection of stories by Jane Yolen, published under the title *Merlin's Booke* (1986), which has great diversity, but lacks the coherence of a novel. Only one recent product of imaginative thinking seems to me to illustrate all the faces of Merlin, making it, for me, the definitive portrait to date.

I said imaginative portrait, because it is not a book. But I make no apology for including it here, because in every other way it fits the notion of a fictional retelling. I refer to the film *Excalibur* (1983), directed and co-written by John Boorman and Rospo Pallenburg.

At one time the intention was to call this film *Merlin* and it is the figure of the mage that dominates the action. Here we encounter him in each of his major aspects. As controller of destinies, he engineers the birth of Arthur, the giving of the magical sword, the shaping of the Round Table, and the quest for the Grail. But he is not of human blood and follows the old ways, which, as he tells his pupil Morgana, 'are numberèd'; and, as he tells Arthur later, he is already fading: 'My time is almost over. The days of men are here to stay.' Like Gandalf, when his work is done, he must depart into the West to become 'a dream to some, a nightmare to others.' Throughout the shifting patterns of the film, Merlin emerges, from Nicol Williamson's portrayal, as tetchy, loving, ingenious, amused, surprised. Possessed of god-like powers, vision and cunning, he is all of the Merlins in one. Finally, he is as baffling as ever, escaping before us like smoke, blown across the blood-soaked field of Camlaan. Yet, it is in that dark ending that Merlin reveals himself most clearly. Let Parke Godwin's *Firelord* say it for me. In this scene Arthur is dying – or fading, however one wishes to see it. Merlin appears, as a boy again, juggling with brightly coloured balls:

> 'The coloured balls soared higher, four of them now, five, six. The shimmering boy balanced and timed their flight so skilfully that they moved in a smooth circle like the sun. "Don't they shine, Arthur? Shaped from the finest tomorrows. Not an easy job, you know. Another dreamer to be born in the same old place: where he's needed".
>
> He was my genius, this juggler, always the more impressive part of me. Or was I merely a facet of him, designed to lead and care for men?'

(p. 364)

This is why Merlin will never be forgotten, why he keeps returning, under the guise of such diverse characters as Mr Spock in the television series *Star Trek*, or as Obi Wan Kenobi in the *Star Wars* saga. Even in novels like Lawrence Durrell's *The Revolt of Aphrodite* (1974) or Walker Percy's *Lancelot* (1979) we may detect the figure of the old mage, looming up against the backdrop of contemporary dreams or board-room politics.

Merlin cannot fade. He is too much a part of us all, too deeply

Figure 8   The Flower Maiden

rooted in our hearts and minds and souls. He is as much the Spirit of Britain as Arthur, and it would be hard to imagine one without the other.

In the collection of stories by Jane Yolen, Merlin's story is brought up to date in a most intriguing way. The story is set in the near future, when a group of reporters have been summoned to a news-conference at which it is revealed that Merlin's tomb has been discovered beneath Glastonbury Tor, and that along with the ancient wizard's mummified body is a strange box, which is to be opened by the Prince of Wales under the eyes of the world's press. Each of them sees something different, but one of Celtic origin, McNeil, see more than any – though what, he dare not say:

'Could he tell them that at the moment the box had opened, the ceiling and walls of the meeting room had dropped away? That they were all suddenly standing within a circle of corinthian pillars under a clear night sky. That as he watched, behind the pillars one by one the stars had begun to fall. Could he tell them? Or more to the point – would they believe?

"Light," he said. "I saw light. And darkness coming on." ... Merlin had been known as a prophet, a soothsayer, equal to or better than Nostradamus. But the words of seers have always admitted to a certain ambiguity ...

"My darlings", he said, "I have a sudden and overwhelming thirst. I want to make a toast to the earth under me and the sky above me. A toast to the arch-mage and what he has left us. A salute to Merlin: ave magister. Will you come?"'

John Matthews

MERLIN'S SONG OF THE STONES

'Shall Merlin raise the stones again
Shall Merlin raise the stones?
And shall he send them forth again
And shall he send them forth?

For if he raise the stones again
For if he raise the stones
Shall Merlin come to earth again
And bring the stars to birth again
And bring the stars to birth.

For once he raised the stones to sing
For once he raised them high
Shall he now raise the stones again
Shall he not set them nigh?

For if he raise the stones again
For if he raise the stones
Then shall the stars be lit again
Under the bright sky.

Shall Merlin raise the stones again
Shall Merlin raise the stones?
And shall he send them forth again
And shall he send them forth?

For under earth and over earth
Shall Merlin raise the stones
And in the darkest halls of earth
The Mabon shall find birth again
The Mabon shall find birth.

Shall Merlin raise the stones again
Shall Merlin raise the stones?
And shall he set the stars again
Upon the hills of bone?

For in the halls of stone again
For in the halls of stone
Shall Merlin find the Sleeping One
And bring him forth by day again
And bring him forth by day.

If he not raise the stones again
If he not raise the stones
How shall the age's child be born
How shall the Child find birth?

Shall Merlin raise the stones again
Shall Merlin set them free?
For if the stones are raised again
The sovereign of the earth shall reign
The sovereign reign on earth.

For Merlin comes to raise the stones
For Merlin comes to raise them up
For Merlin comes to break the bonds
That laid them in the earth.

And shall he raise them up again
And shall he raise them up
Shall Merlin raise the stones again
And set them in the Cup?

For Merlin comes again to sing
For Merlin comes again
To sing the stars down from the sky
And set them in the earth again
And set them in the earth.

And he shall raise the stones again
And he shall raise the stones
For Merlin comes to earth again
To raise his ancient bones again
To raise his ancient bones.'

John Matthews
27 July 1985

PART 4
MERLIN AND THE WHEEL OF LIFE

Merlin, King Bladud, and the Wheel of Life

by R. J. Stewart

'Bladud king of Britain had Logres and Albany. He made a university and a study at Stamford, and a flame and his Temple at Bath his city, which university dured to the coming of Saint Augustine, and the Bishop of Rome interdited it for heresies that fell among the Saxons and Britons together mixed....
... In Caer Bladim he made a temple right
   And set a flamyne theirein to gouerne
   And afterwards a Fetherham he dight
   And sett To fly with wings, as he could best discerene,
   Aboue the ayre nothying hym to werne
   He flyed on high to the temple Apolyne
   And there brake his neck, for al his great doctrine.'

Hardynge's Chronicle, 1543

'A certain monk of Malmesbury, Eilmer by name, had in his youth hazarded an attempt of singular temerity. He had contrived to fasten wings to his hands and feet, in order that, looking upon the fable as true, he might fly like Daedalus, and collecting the air on the summit of a tower, had flown for more than the distance of a furlong; but agitated by the violence of the wind and the current of the air as well as by the consciousness of his rash attempt, he fell and broke his legs and was lame ever after. He used to relate as the cause of his failure his forgetting to provide himself with a tail'

William of Malmesbury, *Gesta Pontificum*, 1125

INTRODUCTION

I wish to state at the very beginning of this essay that it is not confined to 'solar mythology' or 'shamanism'. For nineteenth and twentieth century interpreters of myth and legend either anthropological or psychological – solar or seasonal mythology became a great catch-all system, a type of non-explanatory reductionism which labelled material without giving relative understanding. In the latter part of the twentieth century shamanism is used in a similar manner, often being applied (like glue or wallpaper) to subjects and traditions that probably have no connection with shamanism whatsoever.

I shall be making a number of comparisons between Merlin, the less well known figure of King Bladud, and that ancient cyclical pattern and symbol best summarised by the term 'the Wheel of Life'. The comparisons will certainly include solar mythology and primal magical/religious practices similar to Siberian shamanism; but neither of these fascinating subjects are proposed as the origin or explanation for the material compared.

My main argument is that Geoffrey of Monmouth synthesised and developed certain harmonic themes from Celtic tradition, probably from druidic tradition, and certainly from oral tradition. There is nothing startlingly original in this suggestion, as scholars have been making similar proposals since the nineteenth century and a considerable array of research and publication concerning Celtic studies in general now exists. I am of the opinion, however, that certain aspects of the symbolism employed by Geoffrey in his works, particularly in the *Vita Merlini*, show a mystical and magical psychology which is by no means confined to medieval Christian orthodoxy. The general opinion on the matter is that Geoffrey employed his considerable imagination and skill to develop obscure traditional themes which he himself may not have understood.

We may set the question of Geoffrey's personal understanding on one side for the present, as it does not directly affect the matter in hand; his imagination is abundantly evident, but there are so many eminently practical developments of magical psychology in the *Vita* that it cannot be merely a sustained flight of whimsy based upon extensive reading and misunderstanding. I suspect, but cannot offer proof, that Geoffrey may have understood more than modern scholars give him credit for; this essay will show some of the myriad connectives within his work that are revealed by careful examination.

The magical psychology of the *Vita Merlini* has been examined in my book *The Mystic Life of Merlin*; there is no need to repeat this as evidence in our present context. I propose to concentrate in detail upon the curious relationship between Merlin and King Bladud, and their location upon the ubiquitous Wheel of Life, a pattern used throughout the *Vita* by Geoffrey of Monmouth. The reader does not need to be familiar with the total *Vita*, as any relevant sources and contexts will be given wherever necessary.

My inspiration for this comparison comes from the more recent work of another prolific Geoffrey (Ashe) who, during his talk at the 1986 Merlin Conference, published in this book as Chapter One, enabled me to bridge two areas of study which I had already published but had not attempted to fuse together. Back in 1980 I had examined King Bladud as part of my reasearch for *Waters of The Gap*, a book on the Romano-Celtic mythology of Aquae Sulis, Bath. Subsequently I had published two books on Merlin, based upon the *Prophecies* and the *Vita* by Geoffrey of Monmouth. King Bladud appears in the *History of the Kings of Britain* in which the *Prophecies* are encapsulated, and in a short but important passage in the *Vita Merlini* itself. It was Geoffrey Ashe's view of Merlin as a possible title deriving from an ancient British god, similar to Apollo, that convinced me to merge the two areas of research. For Bladud, as I already knew, was also a title rather than a name, and was also associated with Apollo. Could there be some connection between Merlin and Bladud? Would Geoffrey of Monmouth or his bardic sources have been aware of this connection? Did the figure of Bladud reveal any further insights into Merlin? These were the questions that were uppermost in my mind at the time of writing.

THE WHEEL OF LIFE

To reach any understanding of ancient lore, be it mythical, magical or seasonal, we must first realise that it has a strong tendency towards cyclical patterns. However, the cycles are not closed circles or 'complete systems'; such closures are the restrictive fantasies of materialism or narcissistic intellect. We must look, instead, for open-ended patterns or spirals based solely upon various levels of natural experience. 'Experience' ranges from simple seasonal observations to highly refined stellar maps and analogues; it also encompasses a perennial insight into imagination, human consciousness, and the cycles of polarity that exist both individually and communally in terms of human energy and interaction.

We should not necessarily expect to find ancient lore in forms easily accessible to the modern intellect, as much of it derives from cultures with a communication basis very different from that of our own; the difference is noticeable particularly in matters of the visual imagination and oral collective tradition. While collective, often extensive, memory formed the foundation of culture worldwide, it has a decreasing role in modern mechanised or electronic societies. In this sense our consciousness is rapidly devolving and losing both ability and content; such is the price that we pay collectively for advances in *exteriorising* knowledge and information. The argument is complex and probably insoluble through debate or discussion – only change through time will define the gains or losses.

One of the reasons, often unstated, for the enormous early popularity of Arthurian material is that its sources (such as Geoffrey of Monmouth) formed a significant bridge between oral collective imaginative tradition and the written form. If we are to recover the roots of lore relating to Merlin, we must cross such bridges, recover whatever lies on the other side, and reformulate it in modern terms. Perhaps Geoffrey in his own time and culture did exactly this.

When we examine old tales, myths, magical or psychological expositions and similar source material, we should consider them in the light of cyclical patterns inherent to pre-materialist worldviews. But we should not use such patterns as definitive or restrictive tools for rule-of-thumb interpretation or reduction. With this major con-

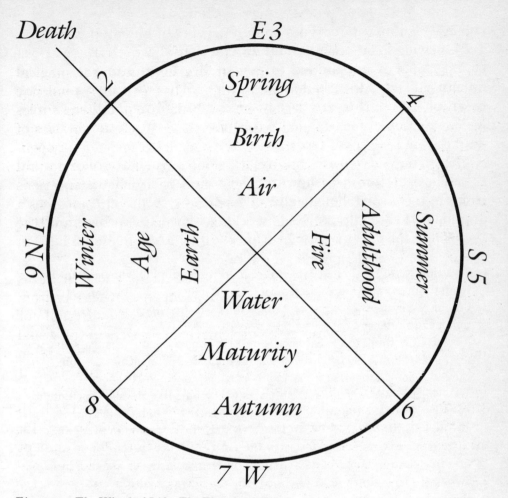

Figure 9   The Wheel of Life: The Elements, The Seasons, and Nine Transformations.

sideration in mind, we can examine the Wheel of Life, which is a central symbol in the legend of Merlin, and is later to be found in literature, expanded from oral magical and mystical traditions. Expressions of the Wheel of Life range from cosmic and apocalyptic vision to the construction of the Arthurian Round Table.

One of the most profound expositions of the Wheel is Geoffrey of Monmouth's *Vita Merlini*, written in elegant Latin verse in about 1150. This text incorporates many Celtic traditional elements fused with classical mythology, cosmology, cosmography and natural history. The *Vita* also develops a refined system of elemental psychology, defining stereotypes and archetypes of human personality, and showing relationships and interactions between the various types. But it is not limited to personality by any means, for the human subjects, described as various characters within a rambling biography of Merlin, are clearly linked to god and goddess forms which are sometimes named explicitly or at other times merely described in functional terms.

The human adventures and relationships which are placed upon the Wheel of Life are shown to be reflections of a macrocosmic pattern that runs holistically (or perhaps we might say holographically) through a series of worlds attuned to a primal fourfold cycle, described in this extract from the *Vita Merlini*:

'Meanwhile Taliesin had come to see Merlin the prophet who had sent for him to find out what wind or rainstorm was coming up, for both together were drawing near and the clouds were thickening. He drew the following illustrations under the guidance of Minerva his associate.

"Out of nothing the Creator of the world produced four elements that they might be the prior cause as well as the material for creating all things when they were joined together in harmony: the heaven which He adorned with stars and which stands on high and embraces everything like the shell surrounding a nut; then He made the air, fit for forming sounds, through the medium of which day and night present the stars; the sea which girds the land in four circles, and with its mighty refluence so strikes the air as to generate the winds which are said to be four in number. As a foundation He placed the earth, standing by its own strength and not lightly moved, which is divided into five parts, whereof the middle one is not habitable because of the heat and the two furthest are shunned because of their cold. To the last two He gave a moderate temperature and these are inhabited by men and birds and herds of wild beasts. He added clouds to the sky so that they might furnish sudden showers to make the fruits of the trees and of the ground grow with their gentle sprinkling. With the help of the sun these are filled like water skins from the rivers by a hidden law, and then, rising through the upper air, they pour out the water they have taken up, driven by the force of the winds. From them come rainstorms, snow, and round hail when the cold damp wind breathes out its blasts which, penetrating the clouds, drive out the streams just as they make them. Each of the winds takes to itself a nature of its own from its proximity to the zone where it is born. Beyond the firmament in which He fixed the shining stars He placed the ethereal heaven and gave it as a habitation to troops of angels whom the worthy contemplation and marvellous sweetness of God refresh throughout the ages. This also He adorned with stars and the shining sun, laying down the law, by which the star should run within fixed limits through the part of heaven entrusted to it. He afterwards placed beneath this the airy heavens, shining with the lunar body, which throughout their high places abound in troops of spirits who sympathize or rejoice with us as things go well or ill. They are accustomed to carry the prayers of men through the air and to beseech God to have mercy on them, and to bring back intimations of God's will, either in dreams or by voice or by other signs, through doing which they become wise. The space below the moon abounds in daemons, who are skilled to cheat and deceive and tempt us; often they assume a body made of air and appear to us and many things often follow. They even hold intercourse with women and make them pregnant, generating in an unholy manner. So therefore He made the heavens to be inhabited by three orders of spirits that each one might look out for something and renew the world from the renewed seed of things." '

Vita Merlini, trans. J. J. Parry.

From the Four Original Powers, which are expressions of the consciousness of divinity, the *Vita* eventually defines Four Seasons upon the planet Earth. This seasonal and Elemental system is the basis for Merlin's adventures. He experiences hardship at Winter alone and mad in the wildwood; he remembers love at Spring in his encounter with Guendoloena, a Celtic Flower Maiden similar perhaps to Blodeuwedd in the *Mabinogion*[1] (notes on p. 145); he undergoes a test of strength at Summer, where he contests wills with a powerful king (his brother-in-law Rhydderch) and is the subject of a ritual drama culminating in the Threefold Death, a sacrificial theme central to Celtic myth and religion[2]. In the Autumn he learns to balance his energies and begins to benefit from the fruits of his experience, guided by his sister Ganieda. In the development of the *Vita* Merlin travels around the Wheel more than once . . . and sometimes there are vast encyclopedic educational digressions.

The Wheel of Life, therefore, is connected to Merlin on a number of levels; defined in the *Vita* as follows: Stellar/Solar/Lunar/Natural or Earth. His adventures are attuned to the Seasons, but also incorporate the Elements within his own nature. His madness and fervour is due to an imbalance of Elements, an excess of certain energies, and is finally restored by a curative spring which gushes up from beneath the earth. Significantly, this miracle occurs just as Merlin has learned the pattern of the cosmos; he cannot be whole until he has some comprehension of a transcendant reality.

'While he was speaking thus the servants hurried and announced to him that a new fountain had broken out at the foot of the mountains and was pouring out pure waters which were running through all the hollow valley and swirling through the fields as they slipped along. Both therefore quickly rose to see the new fountain, and having seen it Merlin sat down again on the grass and praised the spot and the flowing waters, and marvelled that they had come out of the ground in such a fashion. Soon afterward, becoming thirsty, he leaned down to the stream and drank freely and bathed his temples in its waves, so that the water passed through the passages of his bowels and stomach, settling the vapors within him, and at once he regained his reason and knew himself, and all his madness departed and the sense which had long remained torpid in him revived, and he remained what he had once been – sane and intact with his reason restored. Therefore, praising God, he turned his face toward the stars and uttered devout words of praise. "O King, through whom the order of the starry heavens exists, through whom the sea and the land with its pleasing grass give forth and nourish their offspring and with their profuse fertility give frequent aid to mankind, through whom sense has returned and the error of my mind has vanished! I was carried away from myself and like a spirit I knew the acts of past peoples and predicted the future. Then since I knew the secrets of things and the flight of birds and the wandering motions of the stars and the gliding of the fishes, all this vexed me and denied a natural rest to my human mind by a severe law. Now I have come to myself and I seem to be moved with a vigor such as was wont to animate my limbs. Therefore, highest father, ought I to be obedient to thee, that I may show forth thy most worthy praise from a worthy heart, always joyfully making joyful offerings. For twice thy generous hand has benefitted me alone, in giving me the gift of this new fountain out of the green grass. For now I have the water which hitherto I lacked, and by drinking of it my brains have been made whole."'

Vita Merlini, trans. J. J. Parry.

The Wheel expresses cosmology, solar mythology and the passage of the Seasons, while the mad Merlin expresses primal nature practices and magic relating to animals, prevision, inspiration, feats of strength and Otherworld encounters. These aspects of solar mythology and of practices similar to shamanism are but two connected parts of a much greater whole. The Wheel is clearly defined upon a number of levels, and Merlin undergoes a series of encounters and transformations which eventually lead him towards an advanced spiritual maturity in which nature-magic is consciously outgrown.

TABLE OF TRANSFORMATIONS FOUND IN THE *VITA MERLINI*		
1) Grief or guilt	North	Earth
2) Compassion	North-East	
3) Disorientation	East	Air
4) Sexual liberation	South-East	
5) Pre-vision	South	Fire
6) Cosmic vision	South-West	
7) Curative transformation	West	Water
8) Liberation from inner powers	North-West	
9) Spiritual contemplation	North	Spirit

Merlin undergoes nine transformations of his consciousness while spiralling around the Wheel of Life. In some cases there may be more than one full circle between each transformation; the positions upon the Quarters and cross-Quarters of the Wheel of Life are idealised locations relating to the Four Elements. In the extended drama of the *Vita* Merlin encounters transformative situations and personal relationships, in which the Elements or Quarters of the Wheel are channelled through certain individuals or adventures[3].

MERLIN, MABON, AND TIME

One of the themes stated by Geoffrey in the *Vita*, and found in his earlier Merlin book, the *Prophecies*, is that Merlin is a figure who encompasses time. In human terms this is resolved through the conclusion of the Vita, in which Merlin has travelled around all levels of the Wheel of Life (which is a spiral) until he has witnessed all things:

'There stands in the wood an oak, rugged and full of years, so worn by the passage of devouring time that its sap fails and it rots through. I saw this tree when it began to grow, and I saw the falling of the acorn from which it sprang, while a woodpecker perched and watched on the branch above. I have watched the acorn grow unaided observing every detail'

Vita Merlini

Merlin retires to spiritual contemplation in his black cloak, the ideal figure of the Hermit.

In the *History of the Kings of Britain*, however, which includes the *Prophecies*, Merlin is a youth endowed with supernatural origins and startling prophetic powers which reach to the end of time in a dramatic apocalyptic vision. In short, his inner abilities fly far beyond his apparent outer age and form; the transcendant power is resolved in the *Vita* by making the Hermit typical of the first-and-last man who has experienced all things. Thus Geoffrey combines the youthful Merlin with the mad Merlin (a mature man) and the aged hermit Merlin. The Three Faces may appear separately or fused into one trans-temporal being. Although scholars frequently show this conflation to be literary, and speculate upon Geoffrey's own understanding of traditional Merlin legends, there is no problem in terms of mythical symbolism or magical and psychological insight. Geoffrey, regardless of any possible literary confusion over Welsh and Scottish legends, has the imagery right.

As has been suggested in Chapter One, and in my own '*Mystic Life of Merlin*' there are connections between Merlin, Mabon the divine child of the ancient Celts, and the image of Apollo who was a god both of the Sun and the Underworld[5]. Geoffrey of Monmouth may well have been aware of these connections; he maintains the tradition of a prophetic youth, and employs certain images which are also found in the *Mabinogion* connected to Mabon[6]. The removal of the child from his mother, which is central to the Mabon myth, is repeated in the early life of Merlin in the *History*. During the mysterious hunt for Mabon, found in the long tale of *Culhwch and Olwen*[7], a number of totem animals are encountered in a sequence using imagery reminiscent of the *Vita*, in which Merlin is associated with wolf, stag, goat and other creatures. In *Culhwch* these beasts clearly state the theme of great age, each creature representing an older race than the preceding one. Only the oldest of them all, the Salmon of Llyn Llyw, knows where the divine child is imprisoned.

In this sequence we may see echoes of the ageing of Merlin, and in both the *Vita* and in *Culhwch* the symbolism of an oak tree is employed.

'The Stag said: When I first came hither there was a plain all around me without any trees but for one oak sapling which grew up to be an oak with a hundred branches. And that oak has since perished, so that nothing now remains of it but a withered stump . . .'

Culhwch and Olwen

Merlin is closely related to the Stag in the *Vita*, as he leads a herd of stags and goats, acting as Lord of the Animals, an important figure in Celtic myth.

'So he spoke and went about all the woods and groves and collected a herd of stags in a single line, and the deer and she-goats likewise, and he himself mounted a stag. And when day dawned he came quickly, driving the line before him to the place where Guendoloena was to be married. When he arrived he forced the stags to stand patiently outside the gates while he cried aloud, "Guendoloena! Guendoloena! Come! Your presents are looking for you!" Guendoloena therefore came quickly, smiling and marvelling that the man was riding on the stag and that it obeyed him, and that he could get together so large a number of animals and drive them before him just as a shepherd does the sheep that he is in the habit of driving to the pastures.

The bridegroom stood watching from a lofty window and marvelling at the rider on his seat, and he laughed. But when the prophet saw him and understood who he was, at once he wrenched the horns from the stag he was riding and shook them and threw them at the man and completely smashed his head in, and killed him and drove out his life into the air.'

Vita Merlini

The *Mabinogion*, as we know them, were set out two hundred years after Geoffrey, but are certainly based upon oral traditions of much earlier date. It seems likely that both the *Vita* and the theme of Mabon in *Culhwch* are based upon an oral tradition. While we cannot restore this oral tradition fully, it appears to be based upon the following elements:

1) A divine child taken from his proper place
2) A sequence of animals and birds encompassing all time and knowledge
3) The recovery of the child and his restoration to his rightful place

These three elements are developed at great length in both the *Prophecies* and the *Vita*, with the additional change of the youthful Merlin into first a mature and then an aged person, representing spiritual development in human terms.

Geoffrey's Merlin, therefore, incorporates the essence of the lost Mabon cycle with added material showing how this cycle manifests itself in human experience. Once again, we find that the spiralling pattern of myth cannot be confined by simplistic explanations; it manifests itself through a series of conceptual and physical levels. A faint echo of Mabon or of Apollonian themes may be found in the *Vita*, where the mad Merlin is soothed by a Messenger playing upon the *crwth* or lyre. In the story this Messenger is crucial to Merlin's return from winter madness: music enables the Prophet to return to civilisation.

> 'The Messenger heard the prophet lamenting, and broke into his lament with cadences played upon the cither (*Crwth* or lyre) that he had brought to charm and soften madness. Making plaintive sounds with his fingers striking the strings in order, he lay hidden and sang in a low voice ... [here the Messenger sings of Merlin's wife Guendoloena, comparing her to goddesses, stars, and flowers]
>
> ... The Messenger sang thus to his plaintive lyre, and with music soothed the ears of the prophet that he might become more gentle and rejoice with the singer. Quickly Merlin rose and addressed the young man pleasantly, begging him to touch the strings once more and sing his song again ... thus little by little was Merlin compelled to put aside his madness captivated by the sweetness of the instrument.'
>
> *Vita Merlini*

A number of connections are recognised between Maponus (Mabon), Apollo, the lyre, and the island of Britain, from both legend and inscription.

Whatever source or sources Geoffrey drew upon, the connections between Merlin and Mabon were somehow defined, possibly taken from a long exposition of mystical, magical and psychological trans-

Figure 10   Lord of the Animals

formation in the form of a dramatic epic. This is certainly the overall design of the *Vita Merlini*, which has additional material from sources contemporary to Geoffrey, in which medieval knowledge of the natural world was listed, drawing upon many classical sources but elaborated by other influences.

It is possible, though unproven, that Geoffrey's audience was familiar with popular tales and songs echoed by themes in the more

123

sophisticated *Vita*, *History* and *Prophecies*. By the twelfth century such material as remained from ancient religious or mythical traditions was in the possession of bards or itinerant entertainers; the enduring oral tradition was upheld in a diffuse form far removed from any concept of formal druidic learning or coherent Mystery instruction. In this last context Geoffrey is particularly important, for he combined diffuse elements from mystical/magical tradition into the exposition of the *Vita*, just as he had previously combined diffuse elements from history or pseudo-history within the *History of the Kings of Britain*.

KING BLADUD

Geoffrey employs another curious and overtly magical person in both the *History* and the *Vita*: King Bladud.

'After Hudibras came his son Baldudus (Bladud) who reigned for twenty years and built the city of Caerbadus now called Bath. In it he built warm baths for the curing of diseases. He made Minerva the deity of these baths and in her Temple placed inexhaustible fires; these never burned down or turned to ashes but when they began to fail became balls of stone. Bladud was a man of great ingenuity who taught necromancy throughout Britain, continually doing wonderful deeds. Finally he made himself wings to fly through the upper air, but he fell on the Temple of Apollo in New Troy, his body being broken into many pieces.'

History of the Kings of Britain, trans. Aaron Thompson

Geoffrey uses the name Bladud in more than one context in the *History*, and a significant reference linking the theme of Bladud/Apollo with that of Mabon/Apollo is found in the character Blegabred or Bladud Gabred (*History*, 3, 19): 'This prince, for songs and skill in all musical instruments excelled all musicians that had come before him, so he seemed worthy of the title of The God of The Minstrels'.

We can see from the above that a number of themes and symbolic elements are shared by both Merlin and Bladud. Before proceeding with comparisons, we should summarise the attributes of King Bladud:

1) He is a prince or king
2) He practises necromancy or magic
3) He is associated with healing springs
4) He is associated with the goddess Minerva
5) He flies through the air
6) He crash-lands upon the Temple of Apollo
7) He may be associated with music, bards, or minstrels ('joculatores')

We should add to this initial list the fact that Bladud has a specific location within the Land of Britain; the hot springs of Aquae Sulis, Bath, in the south west of England[8]. This emphasis upon location is not mere coincidence, for both Merlin and Bladud have specific places in which they reflect the function of an ancient divinity; at the same time both have a non-localised identity or archetypal nature. We shall expore this subject further as we proceed.

Geoffrey, together with his chronicle source for Bladud, is further supported by a local folk tradition from the Bath area, and the hard evidence of the archaeological finds in the Romano-Celtic temple of Sulis Minerva. Before briefly considering the archaeological material, we should examine the folk tale. Here is the complete story of the pigs that lead Bladud: as told by Robert Pierce M. D., in 1713:

'Bladud, eldest son of *Lud-Hudibras*, (then King of *Britain* and eighth from *Brute*) having spent eleven years at *Athens* in the Study of the Liberal Arts and Sciences (that City being in those Days the chief Academy, not only of *Greece*, but of this part of the World also) came home a *Leper*, whither from that hotter Climate he had conversed in, or from ill Diet, or Infection, it doth not appear, those unletter'd times giving down little or no Account of things (though of greater moment) then transacted; but a *Leper* he was, and for that reason shut up, that he might not infect others. He, impatient of this Confinement, chose rather a mean Liberty than a Royal Restraint, and contrived his Escape in Disguise, and went very remote from his Father's Court, and into an untravell'd part of the Country, and offers his Service in any common Imployment; thinking it (probably) likelier to be undiscover'd under such mean Circumstances than greater. He was entertain'd in Service as Swainswicke (a small Village, two Miles from this City) his Business (amongst other things) was to take Care of the Pigs, which he was to drive from place to place, for their Advantage in Feeding upon Beachmasts, Acorns, and Haws &c. the Hills thereabouts then abounding with such Trees, tho' now few, of the two first, remain. Yet there is a Hill, close upon the *South* Part of this City, that still retains the name of *Beachen Cliff*, tho' there is scarcely a Beach-Tree left upon it.

He thus driving his Swine from place to place, observ'd some of the Herd, in very cold Weather, to go down from the Side of the Hill into an *Alder-moore*, and thence return, cover'd with black Mud. Being a Thinking Person, he was very solicitous to find out the reason why the Pigs that wallow in the Mire in the Summer, to cool themselves, should do the same in Winter; he observ'd them farther, and following them down, he at length perceiv'd a Steam and Smoak to arise from the place where the Swine wallow'd. He makes a way to it, and found it to be warm; and this satisfied him that for the Benefit of this Heat the Pigs resorted thither.

He being a *Virtuoso*, made farther Observation; that whereas those filthy Creatures, by their foul Feeding, and nasty Lying, are subject to Scabs, and foul Scurfs, and Eruptions on their Skin, some of his Herd that were so, after a while, became whole and smooth, by their often wallowing in this Mud.

Upon this he considers with himself why he should not receive the same Benefit by the same Means; he trys it, and succeeded in it; and when he found himself cured of his *Leprosie*, declares who he was; his Master was not apt to believe him, at first, but at length did, and went with him to Court, where he (after a while) was owned to be the King's Son, and after his Father's Death succeeded him in the Government, and built this City, and made these *Baths*.'

Several elements in this tale are connected with both Merlin and Mabon:

1) Bladud is a royal person exiled or displaced from his rightful land
2) Totem animals lead him to the therapeutic springs
3) He is cured by magical water
4) He claims his true inheritance.

Bladud's totem animal is the pig, which features strongly in the Mabinogi of *Culhwch and Olwen* as a powerful Underworld beast; in a Welsh poem of early date, we find Merlin addressing a pig as his totem companion, though in the *Vita* he is also associated with both the wolf and the stag[9].

Before comparing Bladud and Merlin further, and defining the areas of symbolism that they share, one interesting detail should be considered: Bladud is not a name but a title. The name 'Vlatos' appears on Belgic coins struck shortly after Caesar's conquest of Gaul. The image upon the coin is a male Celtic head, with tiny wings sprouting from a neck torque, the symbol of royalty. It is a Gaulish king or tribal leader, bearing symbolic wings and royal insignia, who is likely to have been a leader of mercenary troops under Roman rule. The word 'Vlatos' is quite a close rendering of the Celtic pronunciation of 'Bladud' which is likely to have been literally *Vlathus* or *Vlathuth*.

The period between our medieval chronicle of the flying Celtic king and the Belgic coin bearing the words 'Vlatos Atefla' and a winged male head is considerable; but we have another winged torque bearing a head of a major significance which partly bridges the gap. In the late eighteenth century a remarkable male Celtic head was excavated from the silt that covered the ruins of the temple of Sulis Minerva. Popularly and inaccurately known as the 'Gorgon's Head' this image is the apotropaic guardian of the Romano-Celtic Temple. He has long flowing hair and moustaches, a fierce challenging look, and is given a position of prominence upon a pediment showing a star above and the sea and various underworld creatures below him. Significantly, he sprouts a pair of wings from either side of his head, and carries serpents twisted into a design reminiscent (though this is not possible to prove) of a neck torque.

This wholly Celtic figure, placed upon the 1st century pediment of a Romano-Celtic temple, seems to fly through the air and see all. He soars above the underworld (shown by an owl and another uncertain creature); furthermore he is supported by two classical Victories, and surrounded by an oak wreath ... this indicates that he is associated with the theme of the Victorious Sun, a cult that would have been familiar to both Roman and Celt in different forms. Could this figure be the image preserved in the chronicle descriptions of King Bladud?

Also associated with the temple of Aquae Sulis is a carving of Apollo playing a harp (now built into the church tower at Compton Dando, Somerset). Geoffrey equates Bladud and Apollo, while a number of classical references associate Apollo with British folk religion, as described in Chapter One.

BLADUD AND GUARDIANSHIP

It is interesting that Bladud, a figure of distinctly druidic and solar attributes, was the father of King Leir, whose name is connected with that of Llyr, an ancient sea-god. Leir was buried, according to Geoffrey, in an underground chamber beneath the River Soar, dedicated to the God Janus. Janus is the guardian of doors and gateways in classical mythology, and has two, or sometimes four, faces; he appears in the apocalyptic vision of the *Prophecies*, where he guards the gateways of creation under the control of the goddess Ariadne (The Weaver). It seems that a theme of guardianship is connected to Bladud's kingship, just as it is connected to Merlin's function as prophet[10].

In the *Vita Merlini* Bladud appears as guardian of springs and wells, with his consort Queen Aileron (whose name may be derived from the French word for *wings*). The theme of springs and wells leads onto islands, and finally to the Fortunate Isle where the wounded Arthur is taken by Merlin and Taliesin.

'Of all islands Britain is said to be the best, producing in its fruitfulness every single thing ... it has fountains of health giving hot waters which nourish the sick and give pleasing baths, which quickly cure people. These baths were established by Bladud when he held the sceptre of the kingdom, and he gave them the name of his consort queen Aileron ... [*here a long list of islands follows*] The island of apples, which men call The Fortunate Isle, gets its name from the fact that it produces all crops of itself; the fields have no needs of the plough or of farmers and all cultivation is lacking except what nature herself provides ... thither after the battle of Camlan we [*Merlin and the bard Taliesin*] took the wounded Arthur, guided by Barinthus who knew well the ways of sea and stars ...'

In the cosmology and cosmography of the *Vita Merlini*, the island of Britain occupies a sacred or symbolically central location, within which we find King Bladud acting as guardian of the therapeutic springs; we are then told of a series of increasingly fabulous islands culminating in the Fortunate Isles, ruled over by the priestess or enchantress Morgen and her nine shape-changing flying sisters. Bladud once again, as in the *History*, has the role of linking human and non-human realms, or nature and the Otherworld. In Celtic myth, the gates to the Otherworld or underworld were found in wells, springs, or holes in the ground[11]. The curious figure of Barintus, pronounced Barinthus, a guide or supernatural ferryman, carries Merlin and Taliesin with the wounded Arthur, to the Fortunate Isles.

The remainder of this legend is not directly relevant to our present analysis of Merlin and Bladud, but the figure of Barintus bears some relationship to the lineage of Bladud and other divine king-guardians of the land of Britain. The origins of Barintus are discussed in the article by A. Brown which follows this chapter, but a genealogical table reveals some interesting connections.

THE LINEAGE OF KING BLADUD AND THE GUARDIANS OF BRITAIN

RHUD HUDIBRAS

|

BLADUD

|

LLYR

|

BRAN

RHUTH OR RHUD HUDIBRAS, FATHER OF KING BLADUD

His name contains the element *Rud* or *Ruth*, implying the Welsh word *rhod* or Wheel. The wheel is connected to flight through the Irish druid Mog Ruith (meaning 'Son of the Wheel') who flew through the air wearing a feathered cloak. The sun was known as the *Roth Fail* or wheel of light. The term is found again in the Mabinogi which features Arianrhod (silver wheel), a thinly disguised Celtic goddess who later interpreters have equated with the wheeling stars or with specific constellations[12]. She may also be related to the Ariadne, or weaver-goddess, who Geoffrey describes during the apocalyptic vision of the *Prophecies of Merlin*; a goddess who dissolves the cosmos, and is further related to a Gate-keeping or guardian figure who stands before her portals; this guardian is called Janus in the *Prophecies*.

Arianrhod, silver wheel, is the mother of Lleu in the Mabinogion; Lleu means *bright* or *shining*. Like Merlin in the *Vita* he marries a Flower Maiden, and is associated with the sacrificial Threefold Death. Either Geoffrey and his bardic sources have borrowed freely from the source-tale known to us in the Mabinogi of *Math son of Mathonwy* to colour the tale of Merlin, or, as seems more likely, Merlin and Lleu share certain attributes relating to a Celtic solar deity and the ritual sacrifice whereby the land is renewed[13].

Rhud Hudibras is linked to a prophetic Eagle, which uttered verses while he was building the walls of Shaftesbury.

BLADUD, SON OF RHUD HUDIBRAS

Bladud is also associated with the wheel of the sun, in the legend of his illness, regeneration, and flight. His name may mean *bright-dark*, and he acts as the patron of the healing thermal springs under the goddess Minerva. He is also associated with necromancy and the employment of a magical or inexhaustible fire in honour of the goddess. Bladud has the pig as his totem animal.

LLYR, THE SON OF BLADUD

Llyr is related to the ancient sea god, Llyr, or *Manannan ma Lir* in the Irish sagas. He is connected with the horse as a totem animal, in the form of sea horses or waves. The name 'Lir' literally means 'sea'.. In the *History*, we find that Geoffrey has attached a legend in which a Temple of Janus is dedicated to Llyr or Lear, situated under the river Soar. This theme of guardianship and an underwater or underworld location is central to the Celtic pagan religion[14].

BRAN (AND BRANWEN), THE CHILDREN OF LLYR

Bran is a gigantic figure who is able to wade the Irish Sea. Called Bran the Blessed, he carries the minstrels and musicians upon his back, and acts as a bridge for his army to march across. (*Branwen daughter of Llyr*, Mabinogion.) In the latter part of this legend, Bran has his head cut off, and set as a national guardian in the White Hill, now the location of the Tower of London. He fulfilled the role of guardian against invasion until, according to the Welsh Triads[15], Arthur dug up the head out of misplaced duty or pride. Thus in Bran we have the lineage of Bladud, the sea, musicians, guardianship, and the sacred or magical head. The totem animal of Bran is the raven ('Bran' means 'raven').

ARTHUR AND BARINTHUS

The legend of King Arthur being cured in the Fortunate Isle by the priestess and shape-changer Morgen is perhaps the most revealing element in this web of connections; for the wounded king is carried to the magical realm of regeneration by a seer (Merlin), a bard (Taliesin), and a mysterious ferryman ... Barintus. It seems likely that Barintus is a loosely disguised member of the lineage of divine kings or guardians listed above and is, in fact, a sea deity similar to Llyr. Thus the healing of Arthur, another guardian king, is linked to a visionary cosmography in which King Bladud presides over healing springs, while Morgen presides over the Otherworld. Both are flying druidic characters, connected to Celtic deities. Furthermore Barintus exhibits all the evidence of being of the same lineage as Bladud. It seems that Geoffrey or his bardic source is tapping into an ancient tradition dealing with the magical guardians or sacred kingship of the land of Britain, and its close relationship to a divinity of both sea and sun.

BLADUD AND MERLIN

By the twelfth century, we find Geoffrey of Monmouth combining native Welsh or Breton names and terms with Norman French and Latin; his books abound with curious names, puns, and allusions. The Celtic language sources for Geoffrey's characters have been commented upon by various scholars, but there is still a great area of research untouched.

In our present context, however, it is the use of the name Bladud (in varying forms) that is important. When we analyse the name, the legend, and the archaeological evidence, several remarkable connections are obvious. We have already considered Bladud's legend, his connection to the Romano-Celtic temple of Sulis Minerva, and his further appearance as guardian or patron of therapeutic springs in the *Vita Merlini*. We have also touched upon the curious connection between Bladud, Llyr, Bran and the role of divine king or guardian, equated in Geoffrey's Latinised text with the ancient deity Janus, guardian of all doors, turnings, crossroads, and gateways.

If we regard Bladud as a Celtic (Welsh or Breton) name, it suggests a further connection between the various elements described above. Bladud may be derived from two root words; *bel bal* or *bla* meaning Bright, and *dud* or *dydd*, meaning dark. If Bladud or Beldud or Baldudus is one of the many names in Geoffrey's work with either intentional or traditional Celtic language origins, it seems to mean *Bright-Dark* which fits in with the career of the legendary king who flies through the air like the sun, crash lands upon the temple of Apollo, god of the sun and UnderWorld, and is dashed to pieces.

If he is partly related to the sun and the seasons, though this is by no means his sole mythical or magical explanation, the name *Bladud* reinforces the cyclical pattern; displacement, exile, disease; curative powers from beneath the earth; setting up a temple and an eternal flame; practising necromancy and flying through the air; being dashed to pieces on the Temple of Apollo. The cyclical events turn from dark to light and back to darkness; but, even so, this seasonal magical/psychological pattern is not the entire picture.

We noted above the connection between the lineage of Bladud, the role of Guardianship, and the God Janus who appears in both the *History* and the *Prophecies* firstly in connection with King Llyr and an underground temple, and secondly with the apocalyptic vision and a mysterious goddess called Ariadne who unravels the solar system. If we accept that the Welsh or Breton suggestion of Bladud's name as a god-term or functional description is correct, he is a type of Janus figure.

In this curious role, Bladud functions on three spiralling levels of the Wheel of Life:

1) *Personal.* His career as exiled prince, cured and restored, ruling king, and final reaching beyond the earth into flight.
2) *Seasonal.* A cycle from Winter to Spring (exile and illness to cure) on to Summer (kingship, eternal flame) and Autumn (teaching the fruits of his wisdom throughout the land) and finally a new cycle in which he flies, like the sun, to land upon the Temple of Apollo.
3) *Universal* or cosmic. A primal role of combining light and dark, acting as guardian of gates and doorways ranging from therapeutic springs to the cosmic function of creation and dissolution.

CONNECTIONS AND COMPARISONS

The connections between Merlin and Bladud are sufficient for us to compare the two figures directly:

Both partake of the 'lost child' motif: Bladud in his exile and Merlin (of magical origin) taken from his mother by King Vortigern.

Both partake of a seasonal cyclical life adventure.

Both are involved in a ritualised or mythic death motif.

Both are connected to arts of prophecy, magic, and druidic practices.

Both are linked with totem animals: the pig (shared by both figures) and the deer.

Both have links with the fragmentary Mabon cycle found in Welsh legend.

Both are concerned with springs and therapy in individual ways.

Both are kings or princes.

Both are connected with the passing of King Arthur into the Fortunate Isle.

There are, however, a number of features unique to each character, and these are not interchangeable or derived from each other:

Merlin: Is connected to specific prophecies and utterances.

Has a developed human career in the *Vita* and *History*.

Does not fly through the air.

Is not associated with a specific temple site, though there are indications that he has ancient connections with both Maridunum and Stonehenge. It may be significant that Stonehenge is often suggested as the temple of Hyperborean Apollo found in classical references.

Bladud: Is in many respects a more ancient or primal figure, and is nearer to a god-form than Merlin.

Is said to have contracted leprosy, an incurable disease of a wasting nature, but is not associated with madness, grief or suffering.

Is associated directly with the goddess Minerva (or Sulis/ Minerva in archaeological evidence of Aquae Sulis).

Is cured by following a totem animal to hot springs.

Teaches magic and necromancy throughout the land (which Merlin, contrary to modern opinion, does not do in the early sources – he is limited to prophetic utterances, and in the *Vita* to profound magical and spiritual transformations within himself.)

Is not associated with stellar lore, as Merlin certainly is[16].

It seems from all of the above that Bladud is an expression of a very primal and enduring god-form, connected to the sun and the seasons, but with a deeper role as the god who fuses Light and Dark, the god of the Gates or Crossroads. Merlin, however, is a prophet inspired by the powers which Bladud represents; and both are connected to a goddess similar to Brigidda and Minerva, sharing many of the attributes of druidism.

While both characters have localised expressions, Merlin at Maridunum/Carmarthen, and Bladud at Bath/Aquae Sulis, they are not limited to these sites. Merlin appears in connection with various locations in Scotland, and may share with Bladud the classical connection of Stonehenge (built by Merlin) and Apollo (whose temple was the site of Bladud's fall from the sky).

Bladud is further connected with legends of flight which are found throughout the western world, the most famous of which is the classical Greek myth of Icarus, who flew too close to the sun and thus had his wings destroyed. A similar tale is related of the Gnostic Simon Magus who attempted to fly by magic, and of the Irish druid MacRhoth whose name simply means 'Son of the Wheel'. The legend is certainly not limited to Bladud alone, but he is a major expression of it according to the evidence of the substantial temple of Sulis Minerva, which is associated with him in British tradition.

We must remember that when Geoffrey wrote about Bladud, drawing upon earlier traditions and perhaps the third century writings of Solinus, the temple of Sulis Minerva was lost under the accumulated soil and mud of several centuries. It was not re-discovered until the eighteenth and nineteenth centuries, vindicating the traditions attached to King Bladud and his worship of Minerva, set out by Geoffrey and confirming local folklore.

There may be a further connection between Bladud and the River Avon, which loops around Aquae Sulis, suggesting that his mythical role as a flying deity is perhaps more complex than its localised manifestation at Bath. The site of Malmesbury Abbey, also upon the River Avon, was first established in about 635 by a Celtic Irish monk, Maidulph. According to a chronicle written by a Malmesbury monk (*Eulogy of History*, Rolls Series No 9, Vol 1, p. 224) the site was called Caer Bladon at this period. A charter of 675 also states that the site was 'near the river Bladon'.

Bladon, or Bladim, is also the ancient name for Bath, and Caer Bladon or Caer Bladim are names commonly associated with Aquae Sulis and King Bladud in the medieval chronicles. The connection is strengthened by a witty tale recounted by William of Malmesbury in which a monk, one Guilmerius, tried to fly from Malmesbury Abbey tower with artificial wings and crash landed. Is the monastic chronicler here mocking a folk-tale or local legend, similar to that found in the other Caer Bladim further down the River Avon?

CELTIC PRIMAL TRADITIONS

In order to demonstrate the connections between Merlin, Mabon, and Bladud, we should summarise the foundations of British Celtic primal religion, magic, and tradition[17]. These foundational subjects at the roots of Celtic religion are revealed by legend, early literature, folklore, classical sources, and archaeology. Although authorities are often uncertain as to the connections between the various subjects or elements of primal tradition in Britain (and in other Celtic regions of Europe) there is little doubt about the basic units or themes described in our list. Nor is there uncertainty over the essential fusion of these themes; they are undoubtedly connected in a harmonic or cyclical pattern which persisted from the earliest, even prehistoric, times, reaching well into the nineteenth and twentieth centuries in attenuated forms as folklore. The figures of Merlin and Bladud give us some positive clues to the connections between these foundational elements.

RELIGIOUS ELEMENTS

PROPHECY

Prophecy includes prevision, second sight, and possession of divine inspiration.

ANCESTOR WORSHIP

This includes concepts of genealogical magical inheritance, similar, but not identical, to modern definitions of genetics. Thus the essence or spirit of a king, hero, or other person may appear through successive individuals who are descendants. Ancestor worship includes practices which were termed 'necromancy' in the medieval chronicles: a primal religion in which the spirits of the ancestors played a central role in human daily life. This theme is found throughout the ancient world, and is also the foundation of the Greek/Roman religion. All life springs from a mysterious UnderWorld where energies are regenerated and ancestral spirits reside.

THE SACRED HEAD

The head was held in special reverence by the Celts. It was used as an object of worship in primitive times, and later appeared in cult practices associated with stone heads, masks, sacred skulls and similar objects. Magical skulls were preserved for centuries in Gaelic speaking regions, and were still employed for therapeutic purposes as late as the nineteenth and early twentieth centuries[18]. The magical head also appears in a number of folktales, and in the important Mabinogi of *Branwen daughter of Llyr*, in which the head of Bran 'king' or 'leader' acts as a guardian power defending his company against all grief and suffering, and subsequently as a guardian against the invasion of Britain.

SEASONS, STARS, AND CYCLES

The relationship between the seasons and the stellar patterns was central to early cultures. In Celtic legend we have many references to Seasonal patterns, supported by archaeological evidence from the Romano-Celtic period or earlier. It is clear from early sources, ranging from Julius Caesar[19] through to medieval chronicles and tales, that one of the major arts of the druids involved cosmic science; we are not certain of the form that this took, though it seems likely to have been a fusion of stellar, seasonal, and elemental, and was ultimately a reincarnational theory. We also have archaeological evidence such as the Coligny calendar, and the much debated alignments of stone monuments from prehistoric times and cultures preceding the Celts[20].

UNDERWORLD AND OTHERWORLD

A firm concept of another world or series of worlds (connected to Ancestor worship) is found in all Celtic lore. This realm may be under the earth, or across the sea. The UnderWorld is the realm of the powers of life and death in unity, and holds certain magical objects of regenerative power, such as a Cauldron of Immortality. Entrance to the UnderWorld or Otherworld is usually through water, lakes, springs, or wells. These subterranean gates were held in such reverence that, prior to the Roman invasions, vast hoards of offerings were laid up by the Celts in lakes or springs. There is also some evidence that wells or deep shafts were dug solely for religious purposes.

GODDESS AND HEROES

Primal Celtic religion orbited around a goddess figure. It would be too simplistic to say that the culture or faith of the early Celts was entirely matriarchal, but there is no doubt that the most potent and often terrifying divine images were female. Detailed analysis of goddess forms in early literature and from archaeological evidence suggest a triple aspected goddess, though in many cases she appears only in a single role, or sometimes in a multiple role involving six or nine personae. We may summarise this triplicity as:

a) Maiden, sister, virgin; inspirer of human cultural development
b) Lover, partner, fertile power; inspirer of sexuality and procreation
c) Destroyer; mother of life and death, patroness of prophecy

The first aspect of the goddess is typified by Briggidda, a major Celtic goddess later modified into the Celtic Saint Brigit or Bride. She is equated frequently with Athena and Minerva, sharing many attributes and functions. This goddess plays an important role in the story of Merlin, Bladud, and of course of classical heroes and sacred kings.

The second aspect is typified by Venus, in Celtic legend

Blodeuwedd, or Merlin's wife Guendoloena, both sensuous flower maidens. In early Irish tradition the shape-changing role of the goddess is well defined, but by the time of the medieval tales and chronicles drawn from tradition, the aspects tend to separate.

In the *Vita Merlini* the Flower Maiden, despite her alluring and otherworldly beauty, is rejected by Merlin as he grows beyond sexual attraction towards spiritual maturity. This is rather different from a superficial rejection of sexuality, and really shows the soul or spirit moving from one aspect of the Goddess towards another. Significantly it is Merlin's sister Ganieda who plays the role of Minerva, or educator and enabling feminine power, in the *Vita Merlini*.

The third aspect is typified by the Morrigan, a goddess of life and death, and by the mysterious Faery Queen who inspired prophecy and prevision in later Celtic traditions. In the *Vita Merlini* a strange shape-changing figure called *Morgen* rules a magical island where King Arthur is carried to be cured of his wounds.

This goddess of life, death, regeneration, is also found as the *Apple Woman* in the *Vita*, a vengeful character who distributes poisoned fruit beneath a greenwood tree. The fruit, like that of the Fairy Queen and her magical Tree in the ballad of *Thomas Rhymer*[21], brings madness to mere mortals. The fearful triplicity is also found in the *Prophecies* where a goddess transforms the three springs of Life Desire and Death which rise up from the centre of the land.

TOTEM ANIMALS OR BEASTS

A complex enduring relationship between animals, humans and the environment is found in Celtic symbolism. This extends from overt symbols such as zoomorphic decorations through to profound magical interactions. In such interactions, beasts stand for spiritual qualities or for specific energies. Typical examples are the relationship of the crow with the goddess of death and life (the Morrigan), or of the UnderWorld pig found in the Mabinogion, or in connection with King Bladud as we saw above.

It seems likely from the use of animals in tradition, such as the sequence of animals and birds in *Culhwch and Olwen*, which leads progressively to the discovery of the lost child Mabon, that a very active system of animal symbolism relating to the human psyche and to magical arts was fundamental to Celtic culture. Merlin is found addressing a pig in an early Welsh poem, while in the *Vita Merlini* he has a wolf as a companion in the wildwood, and later becomes the leader of a herd of deer and she goats, while riding upon a stag. Certain powers of nature were, and still are, vested in specific animals, typified through their innate characteristics. Gods, goddesses, heroes and clans all had totem (typical and traditionally maintained) animals or birds. This system is still preserved today in an attenuated form in modern heraldry, and some of the primal aspects of totemism have undergone a popularised and frequently confused revival in modern pseudo-paganism.

SPRINGS, WELLS, AND THERAPY

These are closely related to the UnderWorld or Otherworld concepts outlined above. Therapeutic wells and springs are well known in the modern twentieth-century Celtic cultures, where they are often associated with Catholic saints or the Virgin, as orthodox religion replaces the earlier pagan images. It is significant in this context that both Merlin and Bladud have intimate connections with water sources. Merlin gains his prophetic vision by discovering a hidden spring holding two dragons (in Geoffrey's *History*). The sequence shows a clear insight into the relationship between natural sources (springs, wells, underground caverns) and human prophetic powers. Geoffrey is drawing upon an earlier Celtic tradition, which he repeats in the *Prophecies* with a vision of the Goddess of the Land and Three Fountains.

In the *Vita Merlini* a discourse on the pattern of the cosmos leads on to a description of the microcosm of Earth and the four winds and seas. This in turn leads to the subject of the island of Britain, and on to certain mysterious lands which include the Fortunate Island, clearly an Otherworld location. One of the purposes of this vast discourse is to reveal that there are many healing springs, lakes and pools in the world. Thus the scene is set for Merlin's final cure from madness, by the providence of a spring which suddenly appears from deep beneath the ground.

King Bladud, as we have seen, is cured of leprosy by bathing in the thermal springs found flowing at Bath, and becomes a patron of the springs, of therapy, and a worshipper of the goddess Minerva. The little-known Celtic goddess Sul or Sulis is conflated with Minerva in the Romano-Celtic temple on the site. Her name means eye, gap, or orifice, and she is literally the power of the gap through which the waters flow. We find this portal symbolism of a goddess in the apocalyptic vision of the *Prophecies*.

To summarise, we may suggest that springs and water sources are the gates to the UnderWorld; that they are associated with a goddess, and are further associated with a *guardian*, who is usually male. This imagery may extend to a universal vision, as in the *Prophecies*, or may be entirely localised, as at Aquae Sulis.

MYSTERIOUS OR VIRGIN BIRTH

Certain heroes and gods have a mysterious birth; in our present context we may cite Merlin, born of a virgin and spirit or daemon, Mabon born but stolen away, and Apollo, the classical Greek equivalent.

MYSTERIOUS DEATH OR SACRIFICE

The theme of sacrificial death permeates ancient cultures, and has been dealt with at great length by many scholars. The relationship between death, life, the Underworld and rebirth played a significant role in Celtic culture, and is found in many legends which relate to our present theme. In the Mabinogion, *Lleu* undergoes a curious ritualised death which is known generally as the Threefold or Triple Death. The same ritualised death sequence is connected to the Scottish prophet Lailoken, who is identical with the figure of Merlin in many ways.

In the *Vita* this death is laid upon a sacrificial youth, who seems to stand for all mankind, and not directly upon Merlin. We find once again, that pursuit of a totem beast, the stag, plays an important part of the tale, as the youth dies while hunting.

King Bladud, however, flies through the air, like the sun, and crash lands upon the Temple of Apollo. This seems to be a reference or echo of solar and seasonal symbolism; his being dashed to pieces is reminiscent of a widespread myth in which a solar or saviour figure is dismembered to fructify the land. In both the Merlin and the Bladud tales, therefore, there is a theme of death which is connected to other mythical and magical sacrificial matters.

CONCLUSIONS AND DEVELOPMENTS

From all of the foregoing, we may list the following conclusions:

1) There is a connection between kingship and guardianship in British tradition deriving from primal Celtic belief. This connection appears in the twelfth century attached to the figure of Merlin.

2) In literary developments from Geoffrey of Monmouth through to the present day, the hereditary magical role of the king is increasingly attached to the prophet or magician in a manner that is not present in the earliest sources. Originally, we may infer, there was a working relationship between the prophet (symbolised by Merlin) and the king (symbolised by Vortigern or Arthur). The most primal figure that fuses the druidic and regal functions is that of King Bladud, who may indeed derive from a cultural period in which seer/druid/king/god were at one time identical.

3) For the modern student the sequence of imagery should be reversed as follows:

Arthur	High King
Merlin	Prophet
Bladud	God King

We may develop this theme by adding the linear personae such as Rhud Hudibras or Leir, who connect to Bladud, or the lineage of Arthur. In all cases, it is the figure of Merlin who combines the human and divine realms in one individual, due to his mysterious parentage, which is both mortal and immortal.

Arthur is born of mortal parents acting out a mysterious conception rite (the father in disguise), while the lineage of Bladud is

Figure 11   King Bladud

clearly that of immortal or divine beings; Merlin, traditionally said
to be born of a human virgin and a daemon or spirit, bridges the two
realms.

But none of the foregoing is of any value without the root concept
of a feminine power, the goddess of the land. She is explicitly present
in early Irish legends, but later modified to the important pseudo-
classical Minerva found in the works of Geoffrey. A number of other
primal goddess forms are found connected to Merlin: Ariadne, a
weaving goddess; an unnamed figure who encompasses the Land of
Britain and transforms the Three Springs of Life, Desire and Death;

and the mysterious Apple Woman who controls the poisoned fruit of prophetic madness.

To these feminine images may be added personae in the *Vita* who have the dual role of human character and divine archetype: Merlin's sister Ganieda who is a powerful enabling figure steering Merlin's passage around the Wheel of Life; and Merlin's wife or sexual counterpart Guendoloena who has all the attributes of a Celtic Flower or Nature goddess. The first of these two equates to Minerva/Briggidda, while the second equates to Venus/Blodeuwedd.

We must always be aware that imagery and connectives such as those ascribed to Merlin, Bladud, and the Wheel of Life are not merely literary detective work. They are the foundations of a magical transformative tradition which is intimately connected to the environment. The value of such a tradition is not merely one of ancient lore, but has a potential for modern application. Such application may be either crudely political in terms of environmental activism, or more potent and pervasive in terms of individual meditation and inner rebirth.

The modern tendency of turning Merlin into a 'New Age' cosmic stereotype of a wise elder is extremely enervating and misleading; it suggests the ultimate end of the tale without any of the means, methods, or motivations whereby such an end may be brought into human experience. If we examine, even superficially, the source material for Merlin, which ranges from Scottish legends dealing with the prophet Lailoken to the medieval developments of Geoffrey of Monmouth, it is quite clear that he has a strong human element; the pseudo-mysterious spiritualised Elder is certainly not Merlin, whoever else he may be.

It is in this last context that the Wheel of Life is so vitally important to our understanding; only one aspect of Merlin, or one turn of the Wheel, corresponds to the wise elder. This one aspect must be balanced by the spiralling sequence of aspects and adventures under the inspiration of the Goddess, mediated through the archetype of the divine seer-king.

NOTES TO MERLIN, KING BLADUD, AND THE WHEEL OF LIFE

1 *The Mabinogion*, trans. Jeffrey Gantz, Penguin, 1976. Blodeuwedd is found in the story of 'Math Son of Mathonwy'
2 *The Mystic Life of Merlin*, R. J. Stewart, Routledge and Kegan Paul, 1986
3 *Vita Merlini*, trans. B. Clarke, University of Wales, 1973. For a modern analysis of the magical psychology see (2) above, and *Living Magical Arts*, R. J. Stewart, Blandford Press, 1987.
4 *Historia Regum Britanniae*, Geoffrey of Monmouth. Translators include: J. A. Giles, 1844; L. Thorpe, Penguin, 1966.
5 *Apollo* appears in classical mythology as the god of poetry, music, and prophecy; the patron of physicians, shepherds, and the founder of cities. All males suddenly taken from the world by death were said to be struck by the arrows of Apollo. His original home is sometimes said to be Hyperborea, or even the land of Britain, where he is celebrated by song, dance, and the music of the lyre. He is associated with the serpent python, which he slew while just a babe, and with the seat of prophecy at the oracular site of Delphi, in which a priestess presided over a mysterious underground source of inspiration. His symbols and animals are the bow, quiver, plectrum, serpent, shepherd's crook, swan, tripod, and laurel.
6 *Mabon and the Mysteries of Britain*, C. Matthews, Routledge and Kegan Paul, 1986
7 See (1) above
8 *The Waters of The Gap*, B. Stewart, Bath City Publications, 1981
The British King Who Tried to Fly, H. C. Levis, 1919. Reprinted 1973, Bath
9 *The Apple Tree*: see poem on page 147
10 *Janus*: appears in Roman mythology as the deity who presides over all beginnings and endings, hence our derivation of the month January. The first hour of each day was dedicated to Janus, whose title is Father, his festival was the Roman New Year's Day, and he was traditionally said to have been in Italy before the appearance of any other gods. Images of Janus show a figure bearing a sceptre and a key seated upon a glittering throne. He has two faces, youthful and aged, light and dark, looking ahead and behind. Some images of Janus have four faces, one for each Quarter of the World; he is also known as the god of the crossroads. All doors or passages are under the guardianship of Janus, and his primal nature is further supported by the tradition that he was co-ruler with Saturn of the lost Golden Age.
11 *The UnderWorld Initiation*, R. J. Stewart, Aquarian Press, 1985
12 *The White Goddess*, R. Graves, Faber and Faber, 1961
The Prophetic Vision of Merlin, R. J. Stewart, Routledge and Kegan Paul, 1986
13 See (1) and (2) above
14 *Historia*, ii, 14: 'She buried her father (Leir) in a certain underground chamber which she had dug beneath the river Soar, downstream from the town of Leicester. This chamber was dedicated to the god of two faces, Janus. When the feast day of the god came around, all the craftsmen in the town used to perform there the first act of labour in whatever enterprise they were planning to undertake during the coming year.'
15 *The Welsh Triads*, R. Bromwich, University of Wales, 1961
16 See (2) and (12 [Stewart]) for Merlin and stellar lore
17 *Pagan Celtic Britain*, A. Ross, Cardinal, 1974
18 *The Folklore of the Scottish Highlands*, A. Ross, Batsford Press, 1976

19 *The Conquest of Gaul*, Julius Caesar, trans. S. A. Handford, Penguin, 1951
20 *The Stars and the Stones*, M. Brennan, Thames and Hudson, 1983
    The Stone Circles of the British Isles, A. Burl, Yale University, 1976
    Megalithic Sites in Britain, A. Thom, Oxford, 1967
21 See (11) above for analysis of *Thomas Rhymer*

The Apple Tree

Sweet appletree that luxuriantly grows!
Food I used to take at its base to please a fair maid,
When, with my shield on my shoulder, and my sword on my thigh,
I slept all alone in the woods of Celyddon.

Hear, O little pig! now apply thyself to reason,
And listen to birds whose notes are pleasant,
Sovereigns across the sea will come on Monday;
Blessed will the Cymry be from that design.

Sweet appletree that grows in the glade!
Their vehemence will conceal it from the lords of Rydderch,
Trodden it is around its base, and men are about it.
Terrible to them were heroic forms.
Gwendydd loves me not, greets me not;
I am hated by the firmest minister of Rydderch;
I have ruined his son and his daughter.
Death takes all away, why does he not visit me?
For after Gwenddoleu no princes honor me;
I am not soothed with diversion, I am not visited by the fair;
Yet in the battle of Ardderyd golden was my torques,
Though now I am despised by her who is of the color of swans.

Sweet appletree of delicate bloom,
That grows in concealment in the woods!
At break of day the tale was told me,
That the firmest minister is offended at my creed,
Twice, thrice, four times, in one day.

O Jesus! would that my end had come
Before the death of the son of Gwendydd happen on my hand!

Sweet appletree, which grows by the river-side!
With respect to it, the keeper will not thrive on its splendid fruit,
While my reason was not aberrant, I used to be around its stem
With a fair sportive maid, a paragon of slender form.
Ten years and forty, as the toy of lawless ones,
Have I been wandering in gloom and among sprites.
After wealth in abundance and entertaining minstrels,
I have been here so long that it is useless for gloom and sprites
    to lead me astray.
I will not sleep, but tremble on account of my leader,
My lord Gwenddoleu, and those who are natives of my country
After suffering disease and longing grief about the wood of Celyddon,
May I become a blessed servant of the Sovereign of splendid retinues!

Extract from *Four Ancient Books of Wales*, Skene

Barintus

From the Révue Celtique *XXII pp 339 ff by*
Arthur C. L. Brown, 1901

Geoffrey of Monmouth in his *Vita Merlini*[1] (notes on p. 152) written about 1148 introduces Barintus as the pilot who steered the ship in which Arthur was conveyed to the Fortunate Isles. There is no sign that Barintus is a monk, nor is the land to which he is the guide a Christian paradise. The only point insisted on by Geoffrey is that Barintus knew the waters and the stars.

It has been generally assumed[2], without much reflexion, that Geoffrey got his knowledge of Barintus from the well known introductory episode in the *Navigatio Brendani*[3]. A careful examination of the two passages however seems to me to lead to directly the opposite conclusion. In the *Navigatio* 'saint' Barintus is the head of a band of monks, and the voyage to the *Terra Repromissionis* that he undertakes, in company with his 'filiolus' Mernoc, is a reward for his piety. Furthermore the most that can be said is that Barintus suggests to St Brandan the idea of a voyage: he gives no directions for the way, much less acts as a guide or pilot familiar with the sea.

The Barintus episode in the *Navigatio* is useless for the narrative, and obscure and incoherent in itself. It must be a survival of something[4], almost certainly therefore of some Celtic tradition. It seems to me evident that Geoffrey in the *Vita Merlini* has drawn his notion of Barintus from some such tradition and not from the *Navigatio*. Geoffrey could no doubt fabricate a clever story, but it is asking too much to suppose that he would have been at the pains to strip Barintus of his ecclesiastical character and companions, associate him with Taliessin and Arthur, who are not mentioned in the *Navigatio*, and invent for him a *rôle* as pilot which is in accord with what probably must have been his position in Celtic legend.

We have an unmistakable indication of the existence of a Celtic tradition about Barintus. The life of Saint David, which was written in Wales thirty or forty years at least before the works of Geoffrey of Monmouth[5], contains a curious story which, while it agrees with the *Navigatio* in bringing Barintus, here called St Barri[6] into relation with St Brandan, cannot possibly be a mere adaptation from the Latin legend. The incident is in outline as follows: one day St Barri borrowed a horse from St David, and rode it across the sea from Wales to Ireland. After he had gone a long way he met St Brandan who 'super marinum cetum miram ducebat vitam' and the two saints conversed together.

Zimmer in his important study of the St Brandan legend, has compared this incident to other incidents of a similar character in the lives of St David and St Aidan, and has concluded that Barri must have been originally represented as riding a sort of fish or 'sea-horse'[7]. One naturally wishes to know how such a surprising adventure came to be attached to a saint. Zimmer contented himself with an unlikely suggestion[8], and the matter, despite its interest has not since been discussed.

I believe that to understand the source of this adventure one has only to read in the Irish Sagas the accounts of the sea-god Manannán mac Lir. He is regularly represented as riding[9] a 'sea-horse', and he especially frequented the waters between Wales and Ireland[10]. This is precisely the scene of the adventure of Barri and his fellow saints. We seem therefore to be in the presence of a local tradition which has survived after the pagan god, its original hero, has been forgotten[11].

There is probably special reason why this adventure is found attached to Barri. Barri or Barintus was, I venture to suggest, in origin, like Manannán a sea-god[12] who in the Welsh lives and in the *Navigatio* has been changed into a saint.

To suppose that a pagan divinity has been transformed by later legends into a saint, is not as difficult as it may at first seem. There is an excellent parallel in one of the Mabinogion, *Branwen daughter of Llyr*, where we find the old sea-god Bran, a giant who could wade through the sea from Wales to Ireland, called Bran the Blessed (Bendigeit Bran). The Welsh triads explain that he was a saint and the introducer of Christianity into Britain[13].

Zimmer has shown[14] that Barintus is essentially an epithet or surname. It is the Irish *Barrfind*, sometimes written *Finnbarr*, which means 'fair-haired' or more literally 'white-topped'. A name more appropriate for a god of the hoary sea would be hard to find[15].

It seems highly probable then that Barintus was in origin a god of the waters, and by consequence for the early Celts a god of the Land beyond the Waves, the Happy Otherworld. He may have been a fellow deity to Manannán[16], or he may have been a mere manifestation of that god, who, noted for his delight in shape shifting, probably had different names according to his different appearances[17]. In the *Imram Brain*[18], Manannán is called 'the Fair Man' (Fer find) who rides over the 'white sea' (find frismbein muir). In the *Serglige Conculaind*, he is 'the horseman of the maned' (or 'hairy') 'sea' (Marcach in Mara mongaig)[19]. It is not then difficult to suppose that he may have been known by the epithet 'Fair-haired' (Barrind).

Barintus' character as a kind of sea-deity well known in Celtic legend once admitted, the explanation of all that we are told about him works out with convincing completeness.

In the *Life of St David*, St Barri's ride on horseback across the sea is of course simply a survival of the old sea-god's power of riding the billows. The sea-horse has been partly rationalized into an ordinary horse, permitted by the miraculous power of the saint to tread the sea as dry land.

In the *Navigatio Brendani*, the part played by Barintus is quite parallel to that taken by Manannán, or by one of Manannán's fellows, in many Celtic Otherworld tales. In these tales there is regularly an Otherworld messenger, who suggests to the hero the idea of a marvellous journey. Sometimes this mysterious visitor is a prince[20] of the Otherworld. Sometimes only an emissary[21] from such a prince appears. Once at least[22] the hero is persuaded to set out, by the tale of a previous adventurer, who relates his experiences, somewhat as Barintus does in the *Navigatio*.

The Barintus episode, as it stands in the *Navigatio*, forms no integral part of the narrative. It is told quite in the mysterious style[23] of a Celtic Otherworld voyage. One is justified therefore in regarding it as a confused survival of some introductory incident like those just referred to.

In the *Vita Merlini*, Barintus, who steers the ship of Arthur toward the Otherworld, appears to have been in origin then a sea god, a lord of the Land beyond the Waves, who like Manannán in the tale of Ciabhan conducted the voyager thither[24]. Later when his mysterious character was forgotten, he was represented as a pilot, and this was the form of the legend that Geoffrey knew. The rationalization of a sea-god into a famous navigator, is a sufficiently natural process. We have for it one of the closest parallels imaginable. The thing happened very early to the famous Manannán. In the *Glossary of Cormac*[25] we read:

'Manannan mac lir, a celebrated merchant who was in the Isle of Mann. He was the best pilot that was in the west of Europe. He used to know by studying the heavens, i.e. by using the sky, the period which would be the fine weather and the bad weather, and when each of these two times would change. Inde Scoti [the Irish of course] et Brittones eum deum vocaverunt maris, et inde filium maris esse dixerunt, i.e. Mac Lir "son of sea", et de nomine Manandan the Isle of Mann dictus est.'

Substituting Barrind for Manannán, Geoffrey might almost have had these words under his eye when he wrote[26]:

Illuc, post bellum Camblani, vulnere laesum
Duximus Arcturum, nos conducente Barintho
Æquora cui fuerant, et cœli sydera nota;
Hoc rectore ratis, cum principe, venimus illuc.

1 Ed. Michel, 1837, p. 37. Édition San Marte, *Die sagen von Merlin*, 1853, p. 299, verse 930.
2 C. Ferdinand Lot, *Annales de Bretagne*, XV, 534.
3 Ed. Schröder, 1871, p. 3 ff.; Ed. Jubinal, 1836, p. 1 ff.
4 Such is the opinion of Zimmer, *Ztschr. für deutsches Alterthum*, XXXIII, 314. Cf. de Goeje, *Actes du 8ᵉ Congrès des Orientalistes*, I, 1, 48.
5 For this date see Phillimore in *Y Cymmrodor*, XI, 128. The MS. (Vespasian A, XIV, Cottonian, in the British Museum) is a collection of lives of Welsh Saints. It was published by Rees, *Lives of the Cambro-british Saints*, Llandovery, 1853, see pp. 132–133 (translation p. 435). The text of the above incident has been also printed by the Bollandists, *Acta Sanct.*, vol. I for March, p. 44, note d.
6 Cf. Zimmer, Kuhn's *Zeitschrift*, XXXII, 160.
7 *Ztschr. für deutsches Alterthum*, vol. XXXIII, pp. 307–309 (1889). The life of St Aidan is found in the same MS. as that of St. David.
8 Namely, that the episode originated in a misunderstanding by the Irish of a Norse

'kenning' according to which the early Vikings sometimes called a ship a 'sea-horse' (l. c., p. 309).

9   In the *Serglige Conculaind*, Windisch, *Irische Texte*, 1880, I, 225, line 22, he is called the 'horseman of the hairy sea'. Cf. Nutt and Meyer, *The Voyage of Bran*, I, 10 ff.; the story of Ciabhan in the Colloquy, O'Grady, *Silva Gadelica*, I, 177; and the Second Battle of Moytura, *Revue Celtique*, XII, 104: 'groig maic Lir la maur-ainfini'; [numerous as] 'the Son of Ler's horses in a sea-storm'.

10 He was indeed the traditional lord of the Isle of Man, a place dimly confused with the Otherworld, by the ancient Celts dwelling around the Irish Sea. See Henderson, *Fled Bricrend*, Irish Texts Society, II, p. 142.

11 Thus Odin's 'Wild Hunt' survived with King Arthur as its hero. See Freymond, *Artus Kampf mit dem Katzenungetüm*, p. 378–9. (Festschrift Gröber, Halle, 1899).

12 The idea that we have in Barintus a creature of the Otherworld is of course not new. Henri Martin, *Histoire de France*, Paris, 1857, I, 73 conjectured that Barintus was the Welsh Charon who conducted the souls of the dead to the underworld. He brought forward however no reasons for his idea which seems to have been simply an inference from the *Vita Merlini*.

13 See Loth, *Les Mabinogion*, I, 67.

14 *Ztschr. für deut. Alterthum*, XXXIII, 314.

15 The epithet 'find' (white) is so appropriate for a sea-god, that Meyer and Nutt have suggested that the name of Mongan, the son of Manannán, comes from 'Mong-find' (white mane). *Voyage of Bran*, II, 29 note.

16 Finnbarr occurs in the *Colloquy* (O'Grady, *Silva Gadelica*, I, 199) along with Lir and Teigue and in the *Book of Fermoy* (Todd, *Irish MS. Series*. R.I.A. I, 1, 47) along with Manannán as the name of a chieftain of the Túatha Dé Danann.

17 For references to the shape-shifting habits of Manannán see Meyer and Nutt, *Voyage of Bran*, I, 139, 198, etc. Mongan the reputed son of Manannán was really only a rebirth; the god under another name. 'Orbsen', still another name for Manannán was noted by O'Donovan (Translation of Cormac's Glossary, ed. Stokes, 1868, p. 114).

18 *Voyage of Bran* I, 11.

19 See note above.

20 In the *Echtra Cormaic* (Windisch and Stokes, *Irische Texte*, III, 1, 193, ff.) Manannán, in person, lures away Cormac. In the *Echtra Laegaire* (O'Grady, *Silva Gadelica*, I, 256–7) Fiachna himself invites Laegaire to his realm, So Arawn comes to meet Pwyll (Loth, *Mabinogion*, I, 27 ff.). And Abartach, disguised as the Gilla Decair to lure away Dermot (*Silva Gadelica*, I, 257 ff.).

21 e.g. the 'Summoning damsel' in the *Voyage of Bran* (ed. Meyer and Nutt, I, 2, cf. page 142).

22 In the *Serglige Conculaind* (Windisch, *Irische Texte*, I, 218 ff,) where Laeg relates his journey in order to persuade Cuchulinn to set out. Cf. Chrétien's *Ivain*, where it is the tale of Calogrenant, a previous adventurer, that incites the hero to undertake his journey to the marvellous Fountain.

23 Mernoc knows beforehand of Barintus' approach (a common incident in the Otherworld voyage, cf. *Voyage of Bran*, I, 30, § 62), the two embark in a boat that awaits them, and that travels (there is no mention of oars or sails) through a blinding mist to a marvellous land. Cf. the boat of glass in the *Echtra Connla* (Windisch, *Kurzgefasste Irische Grammatik*, pp. 118–120), that of bronze in the *Serglige Conculaind (Irische Texte*, I, 210), the self-moving boat connected with Manannán's land in the story of Becuma (Summary of the *Book of Lismore* by Todd, R.I.A. Irish MS. Series, I, 1, 38) and the mist through which Cormac journeyed to reach Manannán's 'Fort' (*Echtra Cormaic, Irische Texte*, III, 1, 195).

24 In the Colloquy (O'Grady, *Silva Gadelica*, I, 177). Manannán appears to the voyagers

who are on the point of being ship-wrecked in a tempest. He takes them upon a dark-grey steed, which he is riding, and conducts them, and their boat, to Tir Tairngiri.

25 I employ O'Donovan's translation (ed. Stokes, Calcutta, 1868, p. 114) which is based on the text of Stokes, *Three Irish Glossaries*, London, 1862, p. 31. Where the original is in Latin I have allowed it to stand.

26 *Vita Merlini*, ed. Michel, p. 37, verse 930 ff.

PART 5
MERLIN IN THE
SEVENTEENTH CENTURY

Introduction

by R. J. Stewart

The following extracts from *The Life of Merlin Ambrosius: A Chrono-graphical History of all the Kings and Memorable Passages of this Kingdom* are from Thomas Heywood's recreation of Geoffrey of Monmouth's writings and numerous other early chronicles; Heywood could be said to be either one of the last chroniclers (1641) or one of the first creative novelists to deal with Merlin. The book includes a number of cleverly contrived verses, which more or less correspond to Geoffrey's *Prophecies*, and numerous imaginative tales, colourful explanations, all mingled with considerable scholarship.

Three chapters from Heywood are worthy of our attention, both because of his analysis of the nature of prophecy and the character of Merlin, and for his highly colourful account of the fall of King Vortigern and Merlin's first utterance of prophecy:

Chapter 1: An analysis of prophets and prophecy, with a detailed examination of the origins of Merlin and his pagan and Christian counterparts.

Chapter 3: The legend of Vortigern's Tower, leading to the first utterance of prophecy from the youthful Merlin.

Chapter 4: Merlin becomes Vortigern's court prophet and entertainer or illusionist; finally Vortigern meets his doom as was foretold, and Aurelius comes to the throne.

Figure 12   King Vortigern and the Youthful Merlin

The Life of Merlin Ambrosius

The Life of Merlin Ambrosius: A Chrono-graphical History of all the Kings and Memorable Passages of this Kingdom

CONTENTS OF CHAPTER FIRST.

Of the birth of Merlin sur-named Ambrosius, whether he was a Christian or no, and by what spirit he prophecied.

To prophets there be several attributes given, some are called prophetæ, some vates, others videntes; that is, prophets, predictors and seers, and these have been from all antiquity. The name of prophets was, and ought to be peculiar to those that dealt only in divine mysteries, and spake to the people the words which the Almighty did dictate unto them concerning those things which should futurely happen, and such also are called in the holy text seers; but vates was a title promiscuously conferred on prophets and poets, as belonging to them both: of the first were Moses, Samuel, David, Isaiah, Jeremiah, Daniel, and the rest, whose divine oracles were extant in the old Testament, others there were in the time of the gospel, as John the Baptist, of whom our Saviour himself witnesseth, that he was not only a prophet, but more than a prophet; and we read in the Acts of the Apostles, Chap. 11, 27. *And in those days also came prophets from Jerusalem to Antiochia. And there stood up one of them called Agabus, and signified by the spirit, that there should be great famine in all the world, whch came to pass under Claudius Cæsar.* Of the vatical or prophetical poets among the Greeks, were Orpheus, Linus, Homer, Hesiod, &c. and amongst the Latins, Publius, Virgilius, Maro, with others.

But, before I come to enquire in which of those lists, this, our countryman, Merlin, whose surname was Ambrosius, ought to be filed. It is needful that I speak something of his birth and parents. His mother being certain, but his father doubtful, (for so our most ancient Chronologers have left them) that is, whether he were, according to nature, begot by a man and a woman, or according to his mother's confession, that he was conceived by the compression of a fantastical spiritual creature, without a body, which may be easily believed to be a mere fiction, or excuse to mitigate her fault, (being a royal Virgin, the daughter of king Demetius) or to conceal the person of her sweetheart, by disclosing of whose name she had undoubtedly exposed him to imminent danger; and this is most probable. And yet we read that the other fantastical congression is not impossible; for Speusippus, the son of Plato's sister, and Elearchus the Sophist, and Amaxilides, in the second book of his philosophy, affirm in the honour of Plato, that his mother, Perictione, having congression with the imaginary shadow of Apollo, conceived, and brought into the world him who proved to be the prince of philosophers.

Apuleius also, in his book, intitled, De Socratis Dæmonio, of Socrates his Dæmon, or Genius, writes at large, that betwixt the moon and the earth spirits inhabit, called Incubi, of which opinion Plato was also, who saith, That their harbour was between the moon and the earth, in the moist part of the air. A kind of Dæmons which he thus defines: a living creature, moist, rational, immortal and passible, whose property is to envy men; because to that place from whence they were precipitated, by their pride, man by his humility is preferred; and of these, some are so libidinous and luxurious, that sometimes taking humane shape upon them, they will commix themselves with women, and generate children, from whence they have the name of Incubi, whom the Romans called Fauni, and Sicarii; and of such St Augustine, in his book, De civitate Dei, makes mention.

It further may be questioned, Whether he was a Christian or a Gentile? as also by what spirit he prophesied? a Pythonick or Divine; that is, by the devil, who spake delusively in the oracle of Apollo; or by holy and celestial revelation? For the first, it is not to be doubted but he was a Christian, as being of the British nation. This kingdom having for the space of 200 and odd years before his birth, received the Gospel under king Lucius, the first king of this land, by the substitutes of Pope Eleutherius, by whose preaching, the king, and a great part of his people quite renounced all pagan idolatry, and were baptized into the Christian faith. But by what spirit he so truly predicted, is only known to the God of all spirits, who, in every nation and language, pick'd out some choice persons, by whose mouths he would have uttered things which should futurely happen to posterity, according to his divine will and pleasure; and amongst these was this our Merlin.

CONTENTS OF CHAPTER THIRD.

By what miraculous acci-   the combat betwixt the red and
dent young Merlin came to be   the white dragon, and his pro-
known to king Vortigern: of   phecy thereof.

When Vortigern's architectures had caused the hill to be digged, and the foundation to be laid, on which, to erect this new structure, after the weak men had digged the circuit of the place, where the great stones were to be set in order, they were no sooner laid in the hollow of the earth, but they instantly sunk down, and were swallowed up, and no more seen. At which the workmen wondered, and the king himself was much astonished, and the more proofs they made, the greater cause of admiration they had; especially the situation being upon an hill, and no moorish or uncertain ground. Therefore the king commanded a cessation from the work for the present, and sent to the bards and wisards (of which that age afforded plenty) to know a reason of that prodigy, or at least what it might portend; who, being gathered together, and long consulted amongst themselves, and not finding by any natural or supernatural reason, what the cause thereof might be, concluded in the end, to save their credit, and to excuse their ignorance, to put the king off with an impossibility; and when he came to demand of them what they had done in the matter, they returned him this answer, that those stones could never be laid together, or the place built upon, till they were cemented with the blood of a man-child, who was born of a mother, but had no man to his father.

With this answer the king was satisfied, the soothsayers departed from him (not meanly glad that they had put him off, according to our English word, with a flam or delirement) without any disparagement to their art and cunning, who no sooner left his presence, but the king called his servants about him, commanding them to ride and search into, and through all provinces and countries till they could find such a one as the wisards had spoken of, and by fair or foul means to bring the party unto him, but not acquainting him with the cause, but that the king seeing such a one, would send him back richly and bountifully rewarded. Having received this commission (or rather imposition) from the king their master, we leave them to their several adventures, every one of them being sufficiently accommodated for so uncertain a journey.

One of them amongst the rest happened to come to a town or city called Caer-Merlin, which implies Merlin's town or Merlin's borough, which there is no doubt the same which we call to this day Caermarthen, but my author terms it a city; at whose gates the messengers of the king arriving, it happened that a great many young lads were sporting themselves without the walls; and of the company, two of them in gaming fell out, the one young Merlin, the other called Dinabutius, who, amongst other breathing words, cast into Merlin's teeth, that he was but some moon-calf, as born of a mother, who knew not his father: the servant taking notice of this language, presently demanded what he was, and who were his parents? who returned him answer, that for any father he had, they knew none, but his mother was daughter to king Demetius, and lived a votaress in that city, in a nunnery belonging to the church of St Peter: who presently went to the chief magistrates, and shewed his commission from the king, which they obeying, sent both the mother and son under his conduct, to attend the pleasure of his Majesty.

Of whose coming the king was exceeding joyful, and when they appeared before him (both ignorant of the occasion why they were sent for) the king first asked her, if that were her natural son? who replyed that he was, and born of her own body; he then desired to know by what father he was begot? to which she likewise answered, that she never had the society of any one mortal or human, only a spirit assuming the shape of a beautiful young man, had many times appeared unto her, seeming to court her with no common affection, but when any of her fellow-virgins came in, he would suddenly disappear and vanish, by whose many and urgent importunities, being at last overcome, I yielded, saith she, to his pleasure, and was comprest by him, and when my full time of teeming came, I was delivered of this son (now in your presence) whom I caused to be called Merlin. Which words were uttered with such modesty and

constancy, considering withal the royalty of her birth, and the strict-
ness of the order (in which she now lived) that the king might the
more easily be induced to believe that whatsoever she spoke was
truth.

When, casting his eye upon Merlin, he began to apprehend strange
promising things in his aspect, as having a quick and piercing eye,
an ingenious and gracious countenance, and in his youthful face a
kind of austerity and supercilious gravity, which took in him such a
deep impression, that he thought his blood too noble to be mingled
with the dust and rubbish of the earth, and therefore instead of
sentencing him to death, and commanding him to be slain, he opened
unto him the purpose he had to build this castle, and the strange
and prodigious impediments, which hindred the work, then his
assembly of the bards and wisards, and what answer they returned
him of his demand, but bade him withal be of comfort, for he prized
his life (being a christian) above ten such citadels, though erected
and perfected with all the cost and magnificence that human art or
fancy could devise.

To which words, Merlin (who had all this while stood silent and
spoke not a word) thus replied, Royal Sir, blind were your bards,
witless your wisards, and silly and simple your soothsayers; who
shewed themselves averse to art, and altogether unacquainted with
the secrets of nature, as altogether ignorant, that in the breast of
this hill lies a vast moat, or deep pool, which hath ingurgitated and
swallowed all these materials thrown into the trenches. Therefore
command them to be digged deeper, and you shall discover the water
in which your squared stones have been washed, and in the bottom
of the lake you shall find two hollow rocks of stone, and in them two
horrible dragons fast asleep: which having uttered, he with a low
obeisance made to the king, left speaking.

Who instantly commanded pioneers with pickaxes, mattocks, and
shovels, to be sent for; who were presently employed to dig the earth
deep, where the pond was found, and all the water drained, so that
the bottom thereof was left dry, then were discovered the two hollow
rocks, which being opened, out of them issued two fierce and cruel
dragons, the one red, the other white, and made betwixt them a
violent and terrible conflict: but in the end the white dragon prevailed

over the red. At which sight the king being greatly stupified and amazed, demanded of Merlin what this their combat might portend? Who fetching a great sigh, and tears in abundance issuing from his eyes, with a prophetical spirit, made him this following answer:

> Woe's me for the red Dragon, for alach,
> The time is come, hee hasteth to his mach:
> The bloudy Serpent, (yet whose souls are white)
> Implys that Nation, on which thy delight
> Was late sole-fixt, (the *Saxons*) who as friends
> Came to thee first, but ayming at shrewd ends
> They shall have power over the drooping *red*,
> In which the British Nation's figured:
> Drive shall he them into caves, holes, and dens,
> To barren Mountains, and to moorish fens,
> Hills shall remove to where the valleyes stood,
> And all the baths and brooks shall flow with blood.
> The worship of the holy God shall cease.
> For in thilk dayes the Kirke shall have no peace:
> The Panims (woe the while) shall get the day,
> And with their Idols mawmetry beare sway,
> And yet in fine shee that was so opprest,
> Shal mount, & in the high rocks build her nest.
> For out of *Cornwall* shall proceed a Bore,
> Who shall the Kerk to pristine state restore,
> Bow shall all *Britaine* to his kingly beck,
> And tread he shall on the white Dragon's neck.

Then casting a sad look upon the king, as reading his fate in his forehead, he muttered to himself and said,

> But well-away for thee, to *Britaine* deere,
> For I fore-see thy sad disaster's neere.

Which accordingly happened, and that within a few years after, for Vortigern having builded this castle, and fortified it, making it defensible against any foreign opposition, the two sons of Constantine, whom Vortigern had before caused to be slain, assisted by their near kinsman Pudentius, king of Armorica, or little Britain, (where they had been liberally fostered and cherished) passed the sea with a compleat Army, and landed at Totness, whereof when the Britains who were dispersed in many provinces understood, they crept out of their holes and corners, and drew unto their host, which was no small encouragement to the two brothers, Ambrosius Aurelius and Uter-Pendragon, who now finding their forces to be sufficiently able both in strength and number, made their speedy expedition towards Wales, with purpose to distress Vortigern the usurper.

Who having notice of their coming, and not able in regard of the paucity of his followers to give them battle, he made what provision he could for the strengthening of his castle, to endure a long siege, and to oppose the rage of any violent battery, till he might send for supply elsewhere. But such was the fury of the assailants, that after many fierce and dangerous attemps finding the walls and gates to be impregnable; casting into the castle balls of wild fire, with other incendiaries, they burnt him and his people alive, amongst whom not one escaped. Of him it is reported, that he should have carnal society with his own daughter, in hope that kings should issue from them; thus died he most miserably when he had reigned, since his last inauguration, nine years and some odd months. The explanation of the rest of his prophecy, I will leave to the chapter following.

CONTENTS OF CHAPTER FOURTH.

You have heard what the red and white dragons figured, namely, the British and Saxon people, we will now punctually examine the truth of his predictions in the rest. The caverns, corners, mountains, and moorish places, express into what sundry distresses the natives were driven into, by the merciless cruelty of the strangers; by the hills and valleys, shifting places, that there was no difference amongst the poor Britains, between the courtier and the cottager, the peer and the peasant; by the rivers flowing with blood, the many battles fought between the two nations; and that in those days religion and the true worship of God was supprest, happened under Hengist and Horsus, and their posterity. Octa the son of Hengist, who succeeded his father in the kingdom of Kent, Tosa, Pascentius, and Colgrinus, all pagans and princes of the Saxons. For when the Britains, from the time of Eleutherius, whom the Romists write was the fourteenth pope after the blessed St Peter had received the Christian faith under king Lucius, of glorious memory, and had continued it for many years unto that time.

The Saxons, after coming into the land, being then miscreants, laboured by all means to suppress the same, and in the stead thereof, to plant their pagan idolatry, which they accomplished even to the coming of St Augustine, sent hither by pope Gregory; in whose time again it began to flourish and get the upper hand, in the reign of Aurelius Ambrose, and his brother Uter-pendragon, (which is by interpretation the head of the dragon) who succeeded him. By the boar, which should come out of Cornwall, and tread upon the neck of the white dragon, is meant the invincible king Arthur, who vanquished the Saxons, and subdued them in many battles, and was a great maintainer and exalter of the true Christian religion. Of whose begetting and birth, in this our History of Merlin, we shall have occasion to speak hereafter.

As Merlin was plentifully endued with the spirit of divination; so, by some authors, it is affirmed of him, that he was skilful in dark and hidden arts, as magic, necromancy, and the like; and relate of him, that when king Vortigern lived solitary in his late erected castle, forsaken of the greatest part of his followers and friends, and quite sequestered from all kingly honours, he grew into a deep and dumpish melancholy, delighting only (if any delight can be taken therein) in solitude and want of company. To expel which sad fits from him, which might be dangerous to impair his health, he would devise for his recreation and disport, many pleasant fancies to beget mirth, and sometimes laughter, by solacing his ear with several strains of music, both courtly and rural; the sound heard, but the persons not seen, as with the harp, bagpipes, cymbal, and tabret; and sometimes again with the lute, orphorian, viol, sackbut, cornet and organs. Then, to recreate his eyes, he would present him with stately masks and anti-masks; and again, for variety sake, with rustick dances, presented by swines and shepherdesses. And when these grew stale or tedious to his eye or ear, he would take him up into the top of one of his turrets, whereon he should see eagles and hawks fly after sundry games, and what fowl the king liked, they would strike it into his lap, to add to his slender provision for dinner and supper, which gave the king no small contentment.

Sometimes he would have an hare or hart, hunted and chased by a pack of dogs in the air, the game flying, the hounds, with open and audible mouths, pursuing, with huntsmen winding their horns, and following the chase with all the indents and turnings, losses and recoveries; the champaign plains, the woods, and coverts, appearing as visible and natural as if the sport had been upon the firm and solid earth.

Upon a time, being in the king's Summer parlour, who was desirous to be partaker of some novelty which he had never seen; there instantly appeared upon the table a pair of buts and whites in the middle to shoot at, where suddenly came in six dapper, and pert fellows like archers, in stature not above a foot high, and all other members accordingly proportioned, their bows were of the side bones of an overgrown pike; their strings of a small slivy silk, no bigger than the thread of a cobweb, their arrows less than pick-tooths, feathered with the wings of small flies, and headed with the points of Spanish needles, who made a show as if they were to shoot a match three to three, and roundly they went about it. In the middle of their game, there was a shot which rested doubtful; which, as it appeared, the gamesters could not well decide. Then, Merlin called to one of the servants (who had somewhat a big nose) and stood by, and bade him measure to the mark, and give it to the best; to which, while he stooped, and inclined his face, the better to impire the matter, one of the pigmy archers, who had an arrow to shoot, delivered it from his bow, and shot him quite through the nose, at which he started, and the king heartily laughed; (for there was no room to be seen) and the buts with the archers together disappeared.

But when Merlin knew the king's fate to draw nigh, and not willing to partake in his disaster, he fained occasions abroad, and though, with much difficulty, had at length leave to depart, leaving behind him a paper which he put into the king's closet, where, upon occassion, he might easily find, and read this ensuing prophecy.

> Fly from these fatall severall fires o King,
> Which from less *Britain* the two exiles bring:
> Now are their ships a rigging, now forsake,
> Th' *Armoricke* shoares, and towards *Albion* make,
> To avenge their murdered brothers bloud on thee,
> In *Totnesse* road to morrow they will bee,
> The *Saxon* Princes shall contend in vain
> For young *Aurelius* having *Hengist* slain,
> Shall peaceably possesse the *British* throne,
> Striving the opposite Nations to attone.
> He the true faith shall seek to advance on high,
> But in the quest thereof, by poyson die,
> The Dragons head, his brother shall succeed,
> And after many a brave heroick deed,
> By him perform'd, the fates shall strive to waft,
> His soule ore Styx, by a like poysnous draught,
> But those who sent them to th' *Elizian* bower,
> His sonne the Bore of *Cornwall* shall devoure.

This history needs no comment, being so plain in itself by the success thereof; only this much, let me intreat the reader to bear in memory, that that Arthur, figured under the name of Aper Cornubiæ, that is, the Boar of Cornwall, was son to Uter-pendragon, here called the head of the Dragon.

Amongst many brave heroical acts done by this Aurelius Ambrose; after the death of Vortigern, he maintained the middle part of the kingdom of Britain, with all Cambria and Wales, endeavouring to repair all the ruined places in the land, as forts, castles, and citadels, but especially the temples which were much defaced by the pagan idolators, and caused divine service to be every where said in them, and after that, encountered the Saxons in the hill of Baden or Badove, where he slew many of them, and utterly routed their whole army. After which defeat, another Saxon prince named Porthe, with his two sons, landed at an Haven in Sussex, after whom, as some authors affirms, the place is called Portsmouth unto this day, others landed also in several parts of the kingdom, so that Aurelius had with them many conflicts and battles, in which he sped diversly, being for the most part conqueror, and yet, at some times, repulsed and over-set.

Our English chronicles, and others say, that he, by the help of Merlin, caused the great stones which stand till this day on the plain of Salisbury, to be brought in a whirl-wind one night out of Ireland, and caused them to be placed where they now stand in remembrance of the British lords there slain, and after buried in the time of the pretended treaty and communication had betwixt Vortigern and Hengist, as it formerly touched, but Polychronicon and others, ascribe the honour of their transportage to his brother, Uter-pen-dragon, at whose request to Merlin, that miraculous conveyance was performed; which, if by art he was able to do, no question to be made of the truth of those former prestigious feats, in this chapter before remembered.

The Birth of Merlin

INTRODUCTION

The following extracts come from the 1662 edition of *The Birth of Merlin* by ?William Shakespeare and William Rowley: the first drama to expand upon the theme of Merlin. It seems unlikely that Shakespeare had much to do with the script, yet he was certainly well versed in the works of Geoffrey of Monmouth, and it seems almost surprising that he did not produce a first class Merlin play.

The Birth of Merlin, which is essentially a bawdy comedy mixed with highly technical and demanding sets, visions, and dramatic apparitions, is drawn from the same rich traditional mixture as Heywood's *Chronographical History*. Indeed, they were written within a few years of one another, the play being around 1620, while the History was published in 1641. Once again, we find the sparse themes of the chronicles and the later developments of medieval literature opening out into wildly imaginative and entertaining vistas. Nevertheless the ancient themes of mysterious birth, magical arts, and the power of Otherworld beings are clearly stated in the play.

Drammatis Personæ.

THE SCENE BRITTAIN

Aurelius, King of *Brittain*.
Vortiger, King of *Brittain*.
Uter Pendragon the Prince, Brother to *Aurelius*.
Donobert a Nobleman, and Father to *Constantia and Modestia*.
The Earl of *Gloster*, and Father to *Edwyn*.
Edoll Earl of *Chester*, and General to King *Aurelius*
Cador Earl of *Cornwal*, and Suitor to *Constantia*
Edwyn, Son to the Earl of *Gloster*, and Suitor to *Modestia*
Toclio and *Oswald*, two Noblemen
Merlin the Prophet
Anselme the Hermit, after Bishop of *Winchester*.
Clown, brother to *Jone*, mother of *Merlin*
Sir *Nichodemus Nothing*, a Courtier
The Devil, father of *Merlin*
Ostorius, the Saxon General
Otta, a Saxon Nobleman
Proximus, a Saxon Magician
   Two Bishops
   Two Saxon Lords
   Two of *Edols* Captains
   Two Gentlemen
   A little Antick Spirit
Artesia, Sister to *Ostorius* the Saxon General
Constantia
  and   }   Daughters to *Donobert*
Modestia
Jone Goe-too't, Mother of *Merlin*
A Waiting-woman to *Artesia*
Lucina, Queen of the Shades.

Actus II.

Enter Clown, and his Sister great with childe.

Clown. Away, follow me no further, I am none of thy brother, what with Childe, great with Childe, and knows not whose the Father on't, I am asham'd to call thee Sister.

Joan. Believe me Brother, he was a Gentleman.

Clown. Nay, I believe that, he gives arms, and legs too, and has made you the Herald to blaze 'em, but *Joan, Joan*, sister *Joan*, can you tell me his name that did it: how shall we call my Cousin, your bastard, when we have it?

Joan. Alas, I know not the Gentlemans name Brother, I met him in these woods, the last great hunting, he was so kinde and proffer'd me so much, as I had not the heart to ask him more.

Clown. Not his name, why this showes your Country breeding now, had you been brought up i'th City, you'd have got a Father first, and the childe afterwards: hast thou no markes to know him by.

Joan. He had most rich Attire, a fair Hat and Feather, a gilt Sword, and most excellent Hangers.

Clown. Pox on his Hangers, would he had bin gelt for his labor.

Joan. Had you but heard him swear you would have thought.

Clown. I as you did, swearing and lying goes together still, did his Oathes get you with Childe, we shall have a roaring Boy then yfaith, well sister, I must leave you.

Joan. Dear Brother stay, help me to finde him out, I'le ask no further.

Clown. 'Sfoot who should I finde? who should I ask for?

Joan. Alas I know not, he uses in these woods, and these are witness of his oathes and promise.

Clown. We are like to have a hot suit on't, when our best witness's but a Knight 'ath Post.

Joan. Do but enquire this Forrest, I'le go with you, some happy fate may guide us till we meet him.

Clown. Meet him, and what name shall we have for him, when we meet him? 'Sfoot thou neither knowst him, nor canst tell what to call him, was ever man tyr'd with such a business, to have a sister got with childe, and know not who did it; well, you shall see him,

I'le do my best for you, Ile make Proclamation, if these Woods and Trees, as you say, will bear any witness, let them answer; Oh yes: If there be any man that wants a name, will come in for conscience sake, and acknowledge himself to be a Whore-Master, he shall have that laid to his charge in an hour, he shall not be rid on in an age; if he have Lands, he shall have an heir, if he have patience, he shall have a wife, if he have neither Lands nor patience, he shall have a whore, so ho boy, so ho, so, so.

Within Prince Uter. So, ho, by, so, ho, illo ho, illo ho.

Clown. Hark, hark sister, there's one hollows to us, what a wicked world's this, a man cannot so soon name a whore but a knave comes presently, and see where he is, stand close a while, sister.

Enter Prince Uter.

Prince. How like a voice that Eccho spake, but oh my thoughts are lost for ever in amazement, could I but meet a man to tell her beauties, these trees would bend their tops to kiss the air, that from my lips should give her praises up.

Clown. He talk's of a woman, sister.

Joan. This may be he, brother.

Clown. View him well, you see he has a fair Sword, but his Hanger's are faln.

Prince. Here did I see her first, here view her beauty, oh had I known her name, I had been happy.

Clown. Sister this is he sure, he knows not thy name neither, a couple of wise fools yfaith, to get children and know not one another.

Prince. You weeping leaves, upon whose tender cheeks doth stand a flood of tears at my complaint, and heard my vows and oathes.

Clown. Law, Law, he has been a great swearer too, 'tis he sister.

Prince. For having overtook her, as I have seen a forward blood-hound, strip the swifter of the cry ready to seize his wished hopes, upon the sudden view struck with a stonishment at his arriv'd prey, instead of seizure stands at fearful bay,
Or like to *Marius* soldiers, who o'retook
The eye sight killing *Gorgon* at one look,
Made everlasting stand: so fear'd my power
Whose cloud aspir'd the Sun, dissolv'd a shower:
Pigmalion, then I tasted thy sad fate, whose Ivory picture, and my

fair were one, our dotage past imagination, I saw and felt desire.

Clown. Pox a your fingering, did he feel sister?

Prince. But enjoy'd now, oh fate, thou hadst thy days and nights to feed,

Or calm affection, one poor sight was all,

Converts my pleasure to perpetual thrall,

Imbracing thine, thou lostest breath and desire,

So I relating mine, will here expire,

For here I vow to you mournful plants

Who were the first made happy by her fame,

Never to part hence, till I know her name.

Clown. Give me thy hand sister, *The Childe has found his Father*, this is he sure, as I am a man, had I been a woman these kinde words would have won me, I should have had a great belly too that's certain; well, I'le speak to him: most honest and fleshly minded Gentleman, give me your hand sir.

Prince. Ha, what art thou, that thus rude and boldly, darest take notice of a wretch so much ally'd to misery as I am?

Clown. Nay, Sir, for our aliance, I shall be found to be a poor brother in Law of your worships, the Gentlewoman you spake on, is my sister, you see what a clew she spreads, her name is *Joan Go-too't*, I am her elder, but she has been at it before me: 'tis a womans fault, pox a this bashfulness, come forward *Jug*, prethee speak to him.

Prince. Have you e're seen me Lady?

Clown. Seen ye, ha ha, It seems she has felt you too, here'a yong *Go-too't* a coming sir, she is my sister, we all love to *Go-too't*, as well as your worship, she's a Maid yet, but you may make her a wife, when you please sir.

Prince. I am amaz'd with wonder: Tell me woman, what sin have you committed worthy this?

Joan. Do you not know me sir?

Prince. Know thee! as I do thunder, hell, and mischief, wicth, stallion, hag.

Clown. I see he will marry her, he speaks so like a husband.

Prince. Death, I will cut their tongues out for this blasphemy, strumpet, villain, where have you ever seen me?

Clown. Speak for your self with a pox to ye.

Prince. Slaves, Ile make you curse your selves for this temptation.

Joan. Oh sir, if ever you did speak to me, it was in smoother phrase, in fairer language.

Prince. Lightning consume me, if I ever saw thee, my rage o're-flowes my blood, all patience flies me.

Beats her

Clown. Hold I beseech you sir, I have nothing to say to you.

Joan. Help, help, murder, murder.

Enter Toclio, and Oswold.

Toclio. Make haste, Sir, this way the sound came, it was a wood.

Oswold. See where she is, and the Prince, the price of all our wishes.

Clown. The Prince say ye, ha's made a poor Subject of me I am sure.

Toclio. Sweet Prince, noble *Uter*, speak, how fare you sir?

Oswold. Dear sir, recal your self, your fearful absence hath won too much already on the grief of our sad King, from whom our laboring search hath had this fair success in meeting you.

Toclio. His silence, and his looks argue distraction.

Clown. Nay, he's mad sure, he will not acknowledge my sister, nor the childe neither.

Oswold. Let us entreat your Grace along with us, your sight will bring new life, to the King your Brother.

Toclio. Will you go sir?

Prince. Yes, any whether, guide me, all's hell I see,
Man may change air, but not his misery.

Exit Prince Toclio.

Joan. Lend me one word with you, sir.

Clown. Well said sister, he has a Feather, and fair Hangers too, this may be he.

Oswold. What would you fair one.

Clown. Sure I have seen you in these woods e're this?

Oswold. Trust me never, I never saw this place, till at this time my friend conducted me.

Joan. The more's my sorrow then.

Oswold. Would I could comfort you: I am a Bachelor, but it seems you have a husband, you have been fouly o'reshot else.

Clown. A woman's fault, we are all subject to go to't, sir.

Enter Toclio.

175

Toclio. Oswold away, the Prince will not stir a foot without you.
Oswold. I am coming, farewel woman.
Toclio. Prithee make haste.
Joan. Good sir, but one word with you e're you leave us.
Toclio. With me fair soul?
Clown. Shee'l have a fling a him too, the Childe must have a Father.
Joan. Have you ne'er seen me sir?
Toclio. Seen thee, 'Sfoot I have seen many fair faces in my time, prithee look up, and do not weep so, sure pretty wanton, I have seen this face before.
Joan. It is enough, though your ne're see me more.

Sinks down.

Toctio. 'Sfoot, she's faln, this place is inchanted sure, look to the woman fellow.

Exit.

Clown. Oh she's dead! she's dead, as you are a man stay and help, sir: *Joan, Joan,* sister *Joan,* why *Joan Go too't* I say, will you cast away your self, and your childe, and me too, what do you mean, sister?
Joan. Oh give me pardon sir, 'twas too much joy opprest my loving thoughts, I know you were too noble to deny me, ha! Where is he?
Clown. Who, the Gentleman? he's gone sister.
Joan. Oh! I am undone then, run, tell him I did but faint for joy, dear brother haste, why dost thou stay? oh never cease, till he give answer to thee.
Clown. He: which he? what do you call him tro?
Joan. Unnatural brother, shew me the path he took, why dost thou dally? Speak, oh, which way went he?
Clown. This way, that way, through the bushes there.
Joan. Were it through fire, the Journey's easie, winged with sweet desire.

Exit.

Clown. Hey day, there's some hope of this yet, Ile follow her for kindreds sake, if she miss of her purpose now, she'l challenge all she findes I see, for if ever we meet with a two leg'd creature in the whole Kingdom, the Childe shall have a Father that's certain.

Exit.

176

Loud Musick. *Enter two with the Sword and Mace, Cador, Edwin, two Bishops, Aurelius, Ostorius leading Artesia Crown'd, Constancia, Modestia, Octa, Proximus a Magician, Donobert, Gloster, Oswold, Toclio, all pass over the Stage. Manet Donobert, Gloster, Edwin, Cador.*

Dono. Come *Gloster*, I do not like this hasty Marriage.

Gloster. She was quickly wooed and won, not six days since arrived an enemy to sue for Peace, and now crown'd Queen of *Brittain*, this is strange.

Dono. Her brother too made as quick speed in coming, leaving his *Saxons*, and his starved Troops, to take the advantage whilst 'twas offer'd, fore heaven I fear the King's too credulous, our Army is discharg'd too.

Gloster. Yes, and our General commanded home, Son *Edwin* have you seen him since?

Edwin. He's come to Court, but will not view the presence, nor speak unto the King, he's so discontent at this so strange aliance with the *Saxon*, as nothing can perswade his patience.

Cador. You know his humor will indure no check, no if the King oppose it, all crosses feeds both his spleen, and his impatience, those affections are in him like powder, apt to inflame with every little spark, and blow up all his reason.

Gloster. *Edol* of *Chester* is a noble Soldier.

Dono. So he is by the Rood, ever most faithful to the King and Kingdom, how e're his passions guide him.

Enter Edoll *with Captains.*

Cador. See where he comes, my Lord.

Omnes. Welcome to Court, brave Earl.

Edol. Do not deceive me by your flatteries: Is not the Saxon here? the League confirm'd? the Marriage ratifi'd? the Court divided with Pagan Infidels? the least part Christians, at least in their Commands? Oh the gods! it is a thought that takes away my sleep, and dulls my senses so I scarcely know you: Prepare my horses, Ile away to *Chester*.

Capt. What shall we do with our Companies, my Lord?

Edol. Keep them at home to increase Cuckolds, and get some Cases for your Captainships, smooth up your brows, the wars has spoil'd your faces, and few will now regard you.

Dono. Preserve your patience, Sir.

177

Edol. Preserve your Honours, Lords, your Countries Safety, your Lives, and Lands from strangers: what black devil could so bewitch the King, so to discharge a Royal Army in the height of conquest? nay, even already made victorious, to give such credit to an enemy, a starved foe, a stragling fugitive, beaten beneath our feet, so love dejected, so servile, and so base, as hope of life had won them all, to leave the Land for ever?

Dono. It was the Kings will.

Edol. It was your want of wisdom, that should have laid before his tender youth, the dangers of a State, where forain Powers bandy for Soveraignty with Lawful Kings, who being setled once, to assure themselves, will never fail to seek the blood and life of all competitors.

Dono. Your words sound well, my Lord, and point at safety, both for the Realm and us, but why did you within whose power it lay, as General, with full Commission to dispose the war, lend ear to parly with the weakened foe?

Edol. Oh the good Gods!

Cador. And on that parly came this Embassie.

Edol. You will hear me.

Edwin. You letters did declare it to the King, both of the Peace, and all Conditions brought by this *Saxon* Lady, whose fond love has thus bewitched him.

Edol. I will curse you all as black as hell, unless you hear me, your gross mistake would make wisdom her self run madding through the streets, and quarrel with her shadow, death! why kill'd ye not that woman?

Dono. Glost. Oh my Lord.

Edol. The great devil take me quick, had I been by, and all the women of the world were barren, she should have died e're he had married her on these conditions.

Cador. It is not reason that directs you thus.

Edol. Then have I none, for all I have directs me, never was man so palpably abus'd, so basely marted, bought and sold to scorn, my Honor, Fame, and hopeful Victories, the loss of Time, Expences, Blood and Fortunes, all vanisht into nothing.

Edwin. This rage is vain my Lord, what the King does, nor they, nor you can help.

Edol. My Sword must fail me then.

Cador. 'Gainst whom will you expose it?

Edol. What's that to you, 'gainst all the devils in hell to guard my country.

Edwin. These are airy words.

Edol. Sir, you tread too hard upon my patience.

Edwin. I speak the duty of a Subjects faith, and say agen had you been here in presence,

What the King did, you had not dar'd to cross it.

Edol. I will trample on his Life and Soul that says it.

Cador. My Lord.

Edwin. Come, come.

Edol. Now before heaven.

Cador. Dear sir.

Edol. Not dare? thou liest beneath thy lungs.

Gloster. No more son *Edwin.*

Edwin. I have done sir, I take my leave.

Edel. But thou shall not, you shall take no leave of me Sir.

Dono. For wisdoms sake my Lord.

Edol. Sir, I'le leave him, and you, and all of you, the Court and King, and let my Sword, and friends, shustle for *Edols* safety: stay you here, and hug the *Saxons*, till they cut your throats, or bring the Land to servile slavery, such yokes of baseness, *Chester* must not suffer,

Go, and repent betimes these foul misdeeds,

For in this League, all our whole Kingdom bleeds,

which Ile prevent, or perish.

Glost. See how his rage transports him!

Exit Edol. Capt.

Cador. These passions set apart, a braver soldier breathes not i'th world this day.

Dono. I wish his own worth do not court his ruine.

The King must Rule, and we must learn to obay,

True vertue still directs the noble way.

Loud Musick. *Enter Aurelius, Artesia, Ostorius, Octa, Proximus, Toclio, Oswold, Hermit.*

Aurel. Why is the Court so dull? me thinks each room, and angle of our Palace should appear stuck full of objects fit for mirth and triumphs, to show our high content. *Oswold* fill wine, must we begin the Revels? be it so then, reach me the cup: Ile now begin a Health to our lov'd Queen, the bright *Artesia*, the Royal *Saxon* King, our warlike brother, go and command all the whole Court to pledge it, fill to the Hermit there; most reverent *Anselme*, wee'l do thee Honor first, to pledge my Queen.

Her. I drink no healths great King, and if I did, I would be loath to part with health, to those that have no power to give it back agen.

Aurel. Mistake not, it is the argument of Love and Duty to our Queen and us.

Artes. But he ows none it seems.

Her. I do to vertue Madam, temperate minds covets that health to drink, which nature gives in every spring to man, he that doth hold

His body, but a Tenement at will

Bestows no cost, but to repair what's ill,

Yet if your healths or heat of Wine, fair Princes,

Could this old frame, or these cras'd limbes restore,

Or keep out death, or sickness, then fill more,

I'le make fresh way for appetite, if no,

On such a prodigal who would wealth bestow?

Ostorius. He speaks not like a guest to grace a wedding.

Enter Toclio.

Artes. No sir, but like an envious imposter.

Octa. A Christian slave, a Cinick.

Ostor. What vertue could decline your Kingly Spirit, to such respect of him whose magick spells met with your vanquisht Troops, and turn'd your Arms to that necessity of fight, which the dispair of any hope to stand but by his charms, had been defeated in a bloody conquest?

Octa. 'Twas magick, hell-bred magick did it sir, and that's a course my Lord, which we esteem in all our *Saxon* Wars, unto the last and lowest ebbe of servile treachery.

Aurel. Sure you are deceiv'd, it was the hand of heaven, that in his vertue gave us victory, is there a power in man that can strike

fear thorough a general camp, or create spirits, in recreant bosoms
above present sense?

Ostor. To blind the sense there may with apparition of well arm'd
troops within themselves are air, form'd into humane shapes, and
such that day were by that Sorcerer rais'd to cross our fortunes.

Aurel. There is a law tells us, that words want force to make deeds
void, examples must be shown by instances alike, e're I believe it.

Ostor. 'Tis easily perform'd, believe me sir, propose your own
desires, and give but way to what our Magick here shall straight
perform, and then let his or our deserts be censur'd.

Aurel. We could not with a greater happiness, then what this
satisfaction brings with it, let him proceed, fair brother.

Ostor. He shall sir, come learned *Proximus*, this task be thine, let
thy great charms confound the opinion this Christian by his spells
hath falsly won.

Prox. Great King, propound your wishes then, what persons, of
what State, what numbers, or how arm'd, please your own thoughts,
they shall appear before you.

Aurel. Strange art! what thinkst thou reverent *Hermit*?

Her. Let him go on sir.

Aurel. Wilt thou behold his cunning?

Her. Right gladly sir, it will be my joy to tell,
That I was here to laugh at him and hell.

Aurel. I like thy confidence.

Artes. His sawcy impudence, proceed to'th' trial.

Prox. Speak your desires my Lord, and be it place't in any angle
underneath the Moon, the center of the Earth, the Sea, the Air, the
region of the fire, nay hell it self, and I'le present it.

Aurel. Wee'l have no sight so fearful, onely this, if all thy art can
reach it, show me here the two great Champions of the *Trojan* War,
Achilles and brave *Hector*, our great Ancestor, both in their warlike
habits, Armor, Shields, and Weapons then in use for fight.

Prox. 'Tis done, my Lord, command a halt and silence, as each
man will respect his life or danger. *Armel, Plesgeth.*

Enter Spirit

Aurel. Quid vis?

Prox. Attend me.

181

Aurel. The Apparition comes, on our displeasure let all keep place and silence.

Within Drums beat Marches.

Enter Proximus *bringing in* Hector *attir'd and arm'd after the Trojan manner, with Target, Sword, and Barrel-ax, a Trumpet before him, and a Spirit in flame colours with a Torch; at the other door* Achilles *with his Spear and Falchon, a Trumpet and a Spirit in black before him; Trumpets sound alarm, and they manage their weapons to begin the Fight: and after some Charges, the Hermit steps between them, at which seeming, amaz'd the Spirits, and tremble*

Thunder within.

Prox. What means this stay, bright *Armel, Plesgeth?* why fear you and fall back? renew the Alarms, and enforce the Combat, or hell or darkness circles you for ever.

Arm. We dare not.

Prox. Ha!

Plesgeth. Our charms are all dissolv'd, *Armel* away,
'Tis worse than hell to us, whilest here we stay.

Exit all.

Her. What! at a Non-plus sir? command them back for shame.

Prox. What power o're-aws my Spells! return you Hell-hounds: *Armel, Plesgeth,* double damnation seize you, by all the Infernal powers, the prince of devils is in this Hermits habit, what else could force my Spirits quake or tremble thus?

Her. Weak argument to hide your want of skill: does the devil fear the devil, or war with hell? they have not been acquainted long it seems. Know mis-believing Pagan, even that Power
That overthrew your Forces, still lets you see,
He onely can controul both hell and thee.

Prox. Disgrace and mischief, Ile enforce new charms, new spells, and spirits rais'd from the low Abyss of hells unbottom'd depths.

Aurel. We have enough, sir, give o're your charms, wee'l finde some other time to praise your Art. I dare not but acknowledge that heavenly Power my heart stands witness to: be not dismaid my Lords, at this disaster, nor thou my fairest Queen: we'l change the Scene to some more pleasing sports. Lead to your Chamber,
How're in this thy pleasures finde a cross,

Our joy's too fixed here to suffer loss.

Toclio. Which I shall adde to sir, with news I bring: The Prince your Brother, lives.

Aurel. Ha!

Toclio. And comes to grace this high and heaven-knit Marriage.

Aurel. Why dost thou flatter me, to make me think such happiness attends me?

Enter Prince Uter *and* Oswold.

Toclio. His presence speaks my truth, sir.

Dona. Force me, 'tis he: look *Gloster*.

Glost. A blessing beyond hope, sir.

Aurel. Ha! 'tis he: welcome my second Comfort. *Artesia*, Dearest Love, it is my Brother, my Princely Brother, all my Kingdoms hope, oh give him welcome, as thou lov'st my health.

Artes. You have so free a welcome, sir, from me, as this your presence has such power I swear o're me a stranger, that I must forget my Countrey, Name, and Friends, and count this place my Joy and Birth right.

Prince. 'Tis she! 'tis she I swear! oh ye good gods, 'tis she! that face within those woods where first I saw her, captived my senses, and thus many moneths bar'd me from all society of men: how came she to this place, brother *Aurelius*? Speak that Angels name, her heaven-blest name, oh speak it quickly Sir.

Aurel. It is *Artesia*, the Royal Saxon Princess.

Prince. A woman, and no Deity: no feigned shape, to mock the reason of admiring sense, on whom a hope as low as mine may live, love, and enjoy, dear Brother, may it not?

Aurel. She is all the Good, or Vertue thou canst name, my Wife, my Queen.

Prince. Ha! your wife!

Artes. Which you shall finde sir, if that time and fortune may make my love but worthy of your tryal.

Prince. Oh!

Aurel. What troubles you, dear Brother? Why with so strange and fixt an eye dost thou behold my Joys?

Artes. You are not well, sir.

Prince. Yes, yes, oh you immortal powers, why has poor man so

183

many entrances for sorrow to creep in at, when our sense is much too weak to hold his happiness? Oh say I was born deaf: and let your silence confirm in me the knowing my defect, at least be charitable to conceal my sin, for hearing is no less in me, dear Brother.

Aurel. No more, I see thou art a Rival in the Joys of my high Bliss. Come my *Artesia*,
The Day's most prais'd when 'tis ecclipst by Night,
Great Good must have as great Ill opposite.

Prince. Stay, hear but a word; yet now I think on't,
This is your Wedding-night, and were it mine,
I should be angry with least loss of time.

Artes. Envy speaks no such words, has no such looks.

Prince. Sweet rest unto you both.

Aurel. Lights to our Nuptial Chamber.

Artes. Could you speak so, I would not fear how much my grief did grow.

Aurel. Lights to our Chamber, on, on, set on.

Exeunt. Manet Prince.

Prince. Could you speak so, I would not fear how much my griefs did grow. Those were her very words, sure I am waking, she wrung me by the hand, and spake them to me with a most passionate affection, perhaps she loves, and now repents her choice, in marriage with my brother; oh fond man, how darest thou trust thy Traitors thoughts, thus to betray thy self? 'twas but a waking dream wherein thou madest thy wishes speak, not her, in which thy foolish hopes strives to prolong
A wretched being, so sickly children play
With health lov'd toys, which for a time delay,
But do not cure the fit: be then a man,
Meet that destruction which thou canst not flie
From, not to live, make it thy best to die,
And call her now, whom thou didst hope to wed,
Thy brothers wife, thou art too ne're a kin,
And such an act above all name's a sin
Not to be blotted out, heaven pardon me,
She's banisht from my bosom now for ever,
To lowest ebbes, men justly hope a flood,

When vice grows barren, all desires are good.

    Enter Waiting Gentlewoman with a Jewel.

Gent. The noble Prince, I take it sir.

Prince. You speak me what I should be, Lady.

Gent. Know by that name sir, Queen *Artesia* greets you.

Prince. Alas good vertue, how is she mistaken.

Gent. Commending her affection in this Jewel, sir.

Prince. She binds my service to her: ha! a Jewel 'tis a fair one trust me, and methinks it much resembles something I have seen with her.

Gent. It is an artificial crab, Sir.

Prince. A creature that goes backward.

Gent. True, from the way it looks.

Prince. There is no moral in it aludes to her self?

Gent. 'Tis your construction gives you that sir, she's a woman.

Prince. And like this, may use her legs, and eyes two several ways.

Gent. Just like the Sea-crab, which on the Mussel prayes, whilst he bills at a stone.

Prince. Pretty in troth, prithee tell me, art thou honest?

Gent. I hope I seem no other, sir.

Prince. And those that seem so, are sometime bad enough.

Gent. If they will accuse themselves for want of witness, let them, I am not so foolish.

Prince. I see th'art wise, come speak me truly, what is the greatest sin?

Gent. That which man never acted, what has been done Is as the least, common to all as one.

Prince. Dost think thy Lady is of thy opinion?

Gent. She's a bad Scholar else, I have brought her up, and she dares owe me still.

Prince. I, 'tis a fault in greatness, they dare owe many e're they pay one, but darest thou expose thy scholar to my examining?

Gent. Yes in good troth sir, and pray put her to't too, 'tis a hard lesson if she answer it not.

Prince. Thou know'st the hardest.

Gent. As far as a woman may, sir.

Prince. I commend thy plainness, when wilt thou bring me to thy Lady?

Gent. Next opportunity I attend you, sir.
Prince. Thanks, take this, and commend me to her.
Gent. Think of your Sea-crab sir, I pray.

Exit.

Prince. Oh by any means, Lady, what should all this tend to? if it be Love or Lust that thus incites her, the sin is horrid and incestuous; if to betray my life, what hopes she by it? Yes, it may be a practice 'twixt themselves, to expel the *Brittains* and ensure the State through our destructions, all this may be valid with a deeper reach in villany, then all my thoughts can guess at, however I will confer with her, and if I finde
Lust hath given Life to Envy in her minde,
I may prevent the danger; so men wise
By the same step by which they fell, may rise.
Vices are Vertues, if so thought and seen,
And Trees with foulest roots, branch soonest green.

Exit.

Afterword

There can be no conclusions to follow a compendium of this sort, for all the research, suggestions, deductions, outrageous statements and conclusions have been made within each chapter. For the reader who wishes to take his or her appreciation of Merlin further, there are the books by our various authors and contributors; but more important than any amount of written material is actual experience.

Merlin is ultimately a figure who embodies experience; either the uprush of sudden power as a prophetic youth, or the vast experience of a wise man who has learned from hardship and personal encounter something of the truth of his being. In modern terms, Merlin represents the experience of a relationship between humanity and the land, which eventually becomes transformed into the relationship between the individual consciousness and the universe. If we seek to experience such relationships, no matter how unassuming our personal horizons are, we are poetically and spiritually following the path of Merlin.

Upon this path there are many persons, places, concepts, and mysteries; it is significant that Merlin begins with nature but ends with the stars. His vision commenced underground, but reached to the most distant depths of space and time. We have presumed, through our scientific progress, that the stars and star-power are now close within our control; yet Merlin's prevision suggests that abuse of power will lead to ruin ... not the apocalypse of the *Prophecies*, but of the verses that suggest some strange terrible disaster resulting from pride and misuse of natural forces. While the apocalypse is in the hands of the Weaving Goddess, the human disaster is still within our own control.

If we are able, as Merlin does in the legends, to establish a balanced relationship with the land, the seasons, and the environment, we channel the energies of our collective and individual lives in such a way that all arrogance and misuse of power is negated.

Far from being quaint Celticisms or medieval entertainments, the legends and myths of Merlin and the related later cycle of King Arthur and his court, still hold potent insight and transformative experience for anyone who enters upon the quest for truth.

Works Relating to Merlin, AD 900–1857

Date	Title	Author (where known)
900	*Poems*	Attributed to Myrddin
1135	*Prophecies of Merlin*	Geoffrey of Monmouth
1136	*Historia Regum Brittania*	Geoffrey of Monmouth
1150	*Vita Merlini*	Geoffrey of Monmouth
1155	*Prophecies of Merlin*	John of Cornwall
1180	*Pantheon*	Geoffrey of Viterbo
1200	*Merlin*	Robert de Borron
1215	*L'Estoire de Merlin*	(Vulgate Cycle)
1250	*Merlinsu Spa*	Gunnlag Liefson
1260	*Merlinjs Boek*	Jacob von Maelent
1272	*Les Prophecies de Merlin*	
1290	*Der Theure Morlin (The Esteemed Merlin)*	Alberecht von Scharfenburg
1310	*Prose Merlin*	
1320	*La Storia di Merlin*	Paolino Peri
1350	*Seven Sages of Rome*	
1380	*La Estoria de Merlin*	
1390	*Roman de Silence*	Heldris de Cornualle
1395	*Arthour and Merlin*	
1410	*Merlin*	Henry Lonelich
1473	*Mörlin*	
1480	*Le Morte d'Arthur*	Sir Thomas Malory
1590	*Merlijn*	Volsbroek
1590–1596	*The Faerie Queene*	Edmund Spenser
1683	*The Mystery of Ambras Merlin, Standardbarer Wolf, and Last Boar of Cornwall*	
1615	*Don Quixote de la Mancha*	Miguel Cervantes
1588	*The Birth of Merlin*	William Rowley
1644	*England's Prophetical Merlin*	William Lilly
1650	*Merlin, or the British Enchanter*	John Drayton
1610	*Life & Prophecies of Merlin*	Thomas Heywood
1734	*Merlin or the Devil of Stonehenge*	L. Theobald
1831	*Merlin der Wilde*	Ludwig Uhland
1857	*Merlin and Vivien*	Alfred Tennyson
1860	*Merlin l'Enchanteur*	Edgar Quinet
1862	*Myrdhinn ou l'enchanteur Merlin*	Villemarque

Select List of Modern Works about Merlin

Those marked * not discussed in text

Berger, T., *Arthur Rex*, London: Magnum, 1979
Boorman, J. and R. Pallenburg, *Excalibur*, Orion Films, 1981
Bradley, M. Z. *The Mists of Avalon*, N. Y., Knopf, 1982
Cabell, J. B., *Something About Eve*, N. Y., Ballantine, 1971
Christian, C., *The Sword and the Flame*, London, Macmillan, 1982
Clare, H., *Merlin's Magic*, London, Bodley Head, 1953
Cooper, S., *Over Sea, Under Stone*, Cape, 1965
De Angelo, M., *Cyr Myrddin*, Seattle, Gododdin Press, 1979
Drake, D., *The Dragon Lord*, Tim Doherty, N. Y. 1982
Durrell, L., *Revolt of Aphrodite*, Faber & Faber, 1974
Erskine, J., *'The Tale of Merlin & one of the Ladies of the Lake' American Weekly*,
    Feb. 4, 1940.
Godwin, P., *Firelord*, N. Y., Doubleday, 1980
Haldeman, L., *The Lastborn of Elvinwood*, London, Souvenir Press, 1980
Hildebrandt, R. & T., *Merlin & the Dragons of Atlantis*, N. Y., Bobbs Merrill, 1983
Kane, G., & J. Jakes, *Excalibur*, N. Y., Dell, 1983
Lewis, C. S., *That Hideous Strength*, London, Bodley Head, 1945
Mason, C. W., *Merlin: A Piratical Love Story*, London, Neville Beeman, 1986
McIntosh, J. F., *'Merlin'*, *Fantastic* 9 no 3 (Mar 1960, pp 6–49)
Munn, H. W., *Merlin's Godson*, N. Y., Ballantine, 1976
    Merlin's Ring, N. Y., Ballantine, 1974
Newman, R., *Merlin's Mistake*, London, Hutchinson, 1971
    Testing of Tertius, N. Y., Atheneum, 1973
Norton, A., *Merlin's Mirror*, N. Y. Daw, 1975
Nye, R., *Merlin*, London, Hamish Hamilton, 1978
Percy, W., *Lancelot*, London, Heinemann, 1979
Powers, T., *The Drawing of the Dark*, N. Y., Ballantine, 1977
Powys, J. C., *Porius*, London, Macdonald, 1951
Stewart, M., *The Crystal Cave*, London, Hodder & Stoughton, 1970
    The Hollow Hills, London, Hodder & Stoughton, 1973
    The Last Enchantment, London, Hodder & Stoughton, 1979
Tolkien, J. R. R., *Lord of the Rings*, London, Allen & Unwin, 1968
    Unfinished Tales, London, Allen & Unwin, 1980

Trevor, M., *Merlin's Ring*, London, Collins, 1957
Vansittart, P., *Lancelot*, London, Peter Owen, 1978
White, T. H., *Sword in the Stone*, London, Collins, 1938
   Once and Future King, London, Collins, 1958
   Book of Merlin, London, Collins, 1977
Yolen, J., *Merlin's Booke*, N. Y., Ace Fantasy, 1986
Zelazny, R., *The Last Defender of Camelot*, N. Y., Pocket Books, 1980

SHORT INDEX OF WORKS CITED IN MAIN CHAPTERS

Index